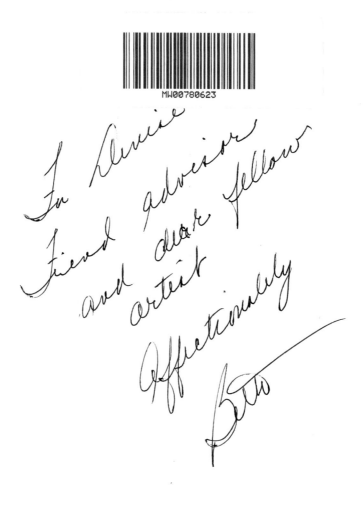

To Denise
Friend advisor
and dear fellow
artist

Affectionately

Beth

To

Dad, Mom, and Father Sherer

In homage and gratitude

Acknowledgments

There are so many to be grateful to and at the top of the list are my five sisters and brother who generously encouraged me, helped edit, shared the memories recorded here and provided their vital support. My special gratitude is offered to my sister, Orietta, who laughed with me as I wrote during her last days with us. We are all less without her. To my daughter, Rachel, for her help, and to my son, John, his mother's deep gratitude for allowing me to depend so heavily on him. Special thanks are reserved for my many friends at the Providence Art Club, including but not limited to: Ann Pipkin, Kathy Simpson, Jane Coie, Carla Rossi, Denise Wall, Philip DeSano, and Lois Atwood for her comments. Thank you to Linda Lazzareschi for her help researching Providence College history; to the Meloccaro family and Fr. Sherer's niece Nancy Hinds and nephew Hal Bochin for their support and approval; to Marilyn DeNardo for her enthusiasm; to Katharine Goddard for her help and encouragement from the start; to Kate Wilson of Ivy Road Design for her assistance in final preparation of the cover and text for print; and to the many others who have read versions of this work for their warm acceptance. I hope everyone knows that they are represented in these pages by their suggestions and that they feel their share of ownership of this book.

For The Love of Pete
and
Father Schnapps

Elizabeth Salzillo

STOCK MARKET FALLS
1929
ENGLAND - GERMANY TALK
1938

Chapter 1

He blew his nose vigorously, and I heard him click on the kitchen light. It was my wake up call. He shut the cabinet door, filled the small, chipped white enamel pan with water, and put it on the stove to boil. He was up and had finished washing. I could get up now. I had waited adrift the swelling thrum of the cicadas. It would be another hot July day.

It is 1943 and a week since my sixth birthday. My name is Elizabeth. They call me Betty. I am tiny for six. Easing out of bed carefully, I picked up the clothes I had set aside the night before. I tiptoed slowly out of the room I share with sisters Clare, age 4, and Mariann, age 2, and moved even more carefully through the adjoining bedroom of Evelyn and Orietta, 12 and 10 respectively. No one seemed to have heard him. That was fine. Taking the stairs quietly and stopping on the wide v-shaped steps at the turn, I dressed. Don't be a pest, I reminded myself, and had learned this was the best time to come down. It was around 5:15.

He was washed and dressed except for his white shirt and was lathering his face. After using it, I knelt on the toilet sideways with my hand and chin on the sink and watched. Nothing was said. We didn't want to disturb Mom and baby Jane nearby. He stroked my hair and pinched my cheek as I wrapped my arms around him with a whispered, "Hi". He didn't talk much ever, and everyone knew he didn't like noisy people, especially loud females. But this was my time. The height of any of my days, it was when I felt like the only child. It was the time when he was not rushed and preoccupied. I was protective of it. He was my father, and I loved him as much as any six-year-old ever could. Intelligent, just, kind, and handsome, he was well respected as a gentleman and engineer. His name is Peter, and he is 36 years old. Craggily built and of medium height, he had a serious and quiet demeanor, soft brown eyes, and gentle reserved disposition.

A dollop of shaving lather from his brush on my nose meant he was finished so I left to put two scoops of coffee in the simmering water. It would steep while he put on his white shirt and loosely knotted tie. His shirt sleeves were folded to the elbows. That was how he always dressed adding the suit jacket when he left the house. He wasn't much interested in clothes other than they are comfortable. Pima cotton shirts with no starch when Mom could find them were his choice.

Dad surveying railroad lines in Florida

People who preened were vain and shallow. You could easily read his discomfort when facing a phony. His measure was one's behavior. "We are known by what we do," he said.

He poured two cups of coffee through the battered tea strainer and a small glass of milk with a spoonful of his coffee for me. One cup he put on Mom's nightstand and gave me a sip from his chunky diner style mug. It was rich, hot, creamy, and sweet.

He went down cellar to his drafting table, and I followed. It was a special place. He had worked the day and evening before drafting plans and visiting city hall records rooms for the jobs planned for today. We watched a while before bed last night as he worked on them. He was tanned from the field work civil engineering entailed. He lit a cigarette and looked over the plan on the table.

The tools of his trade were fascinating —the many-sized triangles; French curves; T-squares; the strange pen with a screw adjusting something that looked like a narrow bird's beak snug in a leather case with blue velvet lining; the boxes of leads with metal ends and their holder, and heavy round sharpener. The Leroy printing set's white rulers of varying point size letters both lower and upper case, and gray stylus ready to slide in the groove was neatly secured in order in a wooden box.   There were squat India ink bottles with rubber dropper tops that had a sort of medicinal smell.

He'd squeeze a drop of the black ink into the set's trolley which moved in a slot in the ruler and in the selected letter. A drop also went into the bird's beak pen. The Leroy set's polished maple box with holes for the different size points was beautiful. He slid the stylus expertly at a speed that seemed reckless but sure. He always had a black ink stain on his index and middle fingers. Even when inking his stamp on the pad, which I opened for him and held firm, as the finishing touch to a drawing, he positioned it carefully in the corner of the drawing. Always perfectly on the mark with even pressure all around the R. I. anchor symbol and professional engineer name and number, it would magically appear to say he had done his best and was ready to deliver it. He was so clever, and I'd watch with a small smile charmed by the rightness of it all.

I loved his letting me be with him so agreeably. Neither he nor Mom seemed to mind any or all of us being quietly at their side for anything they were doing or saying. Around the room were big cardboard tubes with covers filled with past jobs, plans, and maps. There were also shelves with rolls of unused paper. He gave us scraps of one type that when soaked turned to a fine linen cloth for doll's clothes or embroidered hankies.

I broke the silence, "Is Bill coming today?"
"Uh huh." He confirmed.

Great! Bill Maroni would be here soon. He was an MIT Junior in Civil Engineering and son of a neighbor. He wore starched chinos, print shirts with collars, and had horn rimmed glasses. He was nice to me as we sat on the front steps waiting for everyone. He would marry our cousin in years to come. He interned with Daddy when he was needed. That meant the whole crew would be arriving soon. Dad had plot plans spread out and three job books where he entered figures. I took the pencil and spare pad he let us write in, and I mimicked his concentration and tried to copy the neat slanted block printing he used.

I would not ask the question on this busy day. I knew the answer would be the usual, "maybe someday". I wanted to go with the crew in the field. I could help, I thought. They were all friends or relatives and would take care of me. But I understood that he thought this was no place for a girl of any age and certainly not one of his daughters. I asked regularly anyway. He didn't seem to mind. We both smiled. They all returned happy and laughing each day. It seemed like such fun.

Chapter 2

When everyone arrived Dad brought the plans and books out to the garage, and we all followed. He talked to Jim, Phil, and Tony over the plans spread out on the car's hood while the others sawed points on boards to make stakes leaving a pile of wedges. They selected rods, reels of metal measuring tapes, granite bounds, sledge hammers, red plastic streamers, flat pencils, nails, bush hooks, post hole diggers, plumb bobs, machetes, transits (they said guns), and tripods. The transits were packed securely in special wooden boxes with a sturdy leather strap handle on top. These served as perfect tea tables when playing in the garage. We were very careful with them.

Everyone was teasing and joking. One of them would be the butt of the day's ribbing, and this early ritual determined who. It was a happy scene. I guessed a new man named Bob was today's victim. He'd be referred to as Kid or Boy until he showed he had "moxie" to earn his place in the crew.

"We going back to Coventry today?" Artie asked no one in particular while watching Bob. Everyone grinned conspiratorially.

"Yeah, damn it. Have to finish that swampy area. Kid, you'll be clearing brush most of the day so make sure you keep a sharp machete stuck in your boot for the snakes." Jim said. It was an attempt to frighten Bob which seemed to work. He added, "Better take a whetstone too."

Moxie meant that they could take the hardships of the field in stride and the crew's ribbing while carrying their share of the workload. A sense of humor seemed integral to any male group at that time. It put everyone on an equal footing. The better the joke you could tell or funny, self-deprecating personal story you shared, the more solid your position in the group.

In addition to snakes and extreme weather, job hazards included bees, skunks, mosquitoes, gnats, ticks, poison ivy, and nosy irate abutting owners. The poison ivy menace didn't always show itself until after work at home.

Jim had worked for daddy from the beginning and held a leadership position. Phil, Louis, and Artie were uncles, two of them married to Mom's sisters. Jack was Dad's sister's husband. Chris and Mike were cousins. There were other men who came and went as work fluctuated, but these were the regulars. None had come with surveying experience or education except for Bill. Dad trained them and to each a position suitable to his ability was assigned. Promotions were available to the ambitions. Although not openly expressed 'family first' seemed to govern Dad's hiring practices much like Mom's "Play together. That's why I gave you sisters!" did for us.

It was not always without contention. Mom would get calls from her sisters to pass on complaints or demands. She did her best to manage the rancor and hide it from Dad who had no patience with any of it. When he heard of these gripes, his response included epithets such as, "Pit of vipers" and "Selfish goats". Everyone needed work, not least of all Dad who did his best to train and employ family who wanted a job. He had the most mouths to feed and felt deeply a responsibility for all those other families. No one worked as hard as he did and had less rest. They were paid before he was. He often had vicious tension headaches, and we could see the blue vein in his temple throb in confirmation. As his career developed and stresses increased, he suffered not only the headaches but fits of anger. Getting the crews off smoothly would bode well for the whole day.

They would spend the day as early Roman soldiers had when building roads, walls, and aqueducts. The work Dad had done in city hall record rooms located an established, recorded point on the map, and from that point the current survey could start. Civil Engineering field work required a recorded starting point. Finding a granite bound marking that spot would mean an easy start, but locating old stone markers, cairns, walls, or turns in a river would be more difficult. Cutting the brush along lines sighted through the transit and making accurate notations of angles, areas, offsets, and heights was what they were trained to do. They had a book of logarithms which they used. Today with GPS and a theodolite transit with PDA or laptop as data collectors, it is an easier process of triangulation and way to establish the tangents, coordinates, and distances needed to draw a plot plan and write a description of the parcel. This information would be recorded also. Those activities kept Dad busy at home. Structural Engineering calculations would also be done in the office when the project required them.

It was 6:30 when the crews left after loading their cars with equipment. Dad went back downstairs; but Mom was up and made me tend the baby. The long summer day began. It would be as boring and confining as the previous ones. This priceless routine was for summer only. On school days everyone was up, and the winter froze out most of Dad's outside work opportunities. He need not rise so early.

I never did get to go out with the crews but remember the laughter at the end of the day when they turned in their figures and recounted the day's funny moments to Dad who enjoyed this interlude tremendously. However, as the grandsons grew, they were allowed to intern summers as rod or tape boys, which were valuable and cherished times for all of them. I then got some of the funny but often salacious tales my sisters and I were "protected" from as children. Brother Peter ran his own company by this time and added another valued dimension to their experience.

A growing up time for these lucky teens, they shared tales of how an aunt got a very severe case of poison ivy in places which would never be exposed to such an irritant. She required medical attention. There is also a story about one of the crewmen who would wait at the corner of his street for Peter's van to pick him up. When he saw it approaching, he would turn his back, drop his trousers, and moon the van. "Watch him. He's going to moon us," Peter warned. "Jerk thinks that's funny."

A nephew pranked Phil who was driving one day, and from the back seat teased, "Uncle

Phil, do you like seafood?" He replied that he did indeed and then heard, "Eat me, I got crabs." Shaking his head Uncle turned to Peter wearily to say, "What's wrong with kids today!" He took his role as mentor seriously. I doubt those types of jokes would have been tried 30 years before. It was the 70's by then and codes of conduct had really changed, assaulting respect for one's elders as well. A sociable high point to end the week of surveying, Peter would treat the crews to a beer and platter of snail salad.

At times one of the crew would return silent and angry. Dad would notice and want to know why. After some coaxing it would be revealed that the victim had been hazed which could include being left in the woods alone as a prank while the others drove off a distance and waited for their panicked co-worker to emerge from the trees.

Uncle Phil was a favorite of all us children. Fiercely loyal to Dad, he was a big man with a very ruddy complexion. He was teasingly called "mouliniam" which was their pronunciation of eggplant in Italian and used disparagingly at times. To entertain us he had developed his "Chicken Dance". We all loved it and would beg him to sing it, and then would laugh until we fell over while we followed him in imitation. He would tuck his big fists into his armpits and hop around bobbing his head and flapping his wings while singing "Gawkida, gawkida, gawkida" and some other words I never deciphered. Then he would drop to his knees, and we would all jump on him shouting "Gawkida".

There were many strong men and gentle loving ones in our lives to engage and protect, models against which to make judgments in the future.

Today for us there would be chores and challenges. Hanging out the laundry wasn't bad, but washing the two staircases was nasty. Beds were easy. Bathroom scrubbing a daily routine. Ironing a mountain of cotton dresses meant you could be indoors. Clare and Mariann did their best with a dust cloth for now and would take on heavier jobs as they grew. Evelyn and Ori worked by Mom's side and handled a great deal of her work. That might be anything to help her run this large family in this tiny house. We were her "little army", she'd say.

Her health was not always good. Diabetes and serious pregnancy complications often confined her to bed. She needed to nap each day, which meant all of us 'little ones' too, and was torture for me. She would say "just for five minutes". It would be a quiet time off her feet with all of us safely in one place. We napped all together on her bed and were to stay still, no fidgeting. I was a fidgeter, and couldn't stop it. Poor Mom would poke me lightly as a quiet reminder. It didn't work and generally provoked a scolding or slap earning me the nickname "Fidget" for awhile. I regret now that I robbed her of that respite.

She was petite and beautiful with large dark eyes, creamy pink complexion and dark wavy hair. All her health issues combined with very difficult responsibilities for Dad's ill and aging family when they were first married increased her reliance on faith as a source of strength and peace. She had a quiet, reflective demeanor and was very devout. She was 34 years old.

Always very appreciative of anything any one of us would do to pitch in, she explained from her bed how to cook a meal or run an errand and was full of praise for our efforts. Sometimes she would ask us to help one of the neighbors who needed an extra pair of hands or eyes. She would smile proudly when we returned. She didn't drive. When needed she would take the bus 'downcity' to Providence for a day of shopping for those items she wasn't able to order from the Sears Roebuck catalog. On a rotating schedule, a lucky one of us would be selected to accompany her. It was an exciting experience, our Disney World. We visited all the major department stores, and there would be at least one special treat for the fortunate one to pick out. Lunch was always Chinese food at the restaurant on the floor above City Hall Hardware Store on Washington Street. We'd return home laden with bags and boxes and the fun would begin again as everyone received their items and tried everything on.

We didn't receive an allowance, but anything we needed and some of what we wanted was always supplied. Mom would say, "Get my change purse", and milk money, ice cream money, etc. would be dropped into our upturned hands. Bottles had deposits that were ours to collect and return to the small grocer's a few blocks away. That was pretty much the only place to spend money.

We knew the city well by high school age and would be entrusted with as much as five or six hundred dollars in cash to pay bills with after school. The electric and gas companies with cages like a bank, the insurance company on the second floor over a fur store, all the department stores where she used the small metal Charge-a-plate in its little leather sleeve for credit, and the milliner were all on the route and could be covered quickly. None of us ever had the money stolen or lost as we went through the day from class to class. We also knew the what and where of items she would ask us to buy. We were smart shoppers by the time we left for college and married.

JAPANESE BOMB HONOLULU
TOKYO DECLARES WAR
ON U.S. AND ENGLAND
DECEMBER 7, 1941

Chapter 3

World War II raged in Europe. Our lives were changed when Pearl Harbor was attacked. Radios could be heard crackling in every street. People didn't smile readily and were easily drawn into talk of the latest battle. Everything was serious. Everyone was connected by it. A sense of country and patriotism was evident at all times. Speculation on allied or enemy tactics was the hottest topic. Some people seemed to know more than others about ships, planes, maps, etc. and received rapt attention and the reputation of expert on things military and as the one to verify war news and issues.

Everyone had a "we must all pitch in" feeling. Our friends and family did their share. As little girls we couldn't do much but liked Victory Garden work. Watering and weeding were sort of fun. Most homes had a backyard garden to add to their food ration. Mom jumped wholeheartedly into the effort. It would help feed her family, and she would do it right or not at all. We learned canning, or jarring, as some called it.

Relatives and neighbors swapped recipes and relayed stories of their successes and disappointments. Uncles and neighbors shared seeds and plants. Mom would show guests down to the preserve cellar (a scary place under the cellar steps) with its shelves that Dad installed.

It was a pretty sight. Sparkling clean jars of colorful vegetables and fruits were lined neatly by size. With little sugar for baking, it was not unusual for guests to bring a preserve of some sort when visiting and be sent home with one or with a share of produce. Sick visits also meant a jar of something instead of flowers or candy.

Mom went back to school to learn her recipes and techniques at classes she attended at the gas company. Their Lady-in-White would encourage and teach. Brochures came each day if not in the morning mail delivery then later in the afternoon one. It was a very successful program for that company and united every household in a common patriotic effort. This was something we could do. Everyone had brothers or sons in uniform. Men from Dad's crews were called up or volunteered. The Italian representation was one of the largest ethnic groups in America's forces.

When all the produce from our small garden was canned, Mom bought bushels of grapes for jelly, peppers for relish and pickling, spinach and

Swiss chard to steam and pack, watermelon for rind relish, bushels of pears, peaches, grapes, etc. for fruit cocktail, ruby red tomatoes with basil packed in large jars, and syrupy golden slices of peaches. She completed the summer's production display by purchasing an imported cured Parma ham in white tissue paper with green and red lettering to hang in the center of the locker. We had all helped in the summer kitchen in the basement.

Mom managed her kitchen like a conductor and used her chin to indicate where something was, whether to go upstairs, to get behind her, or where to put something, and in response to our questions. Her concentration was total and this nod worked better than continual verbal interruptions. If she got angry we fled especially if she reached for the wooden spoon. Her most dire warning was biting her hand and flaring her eyes. It never lasted long. She must have needed us too much for "time outs", and the return to her good graces was something we needed more. I can see her still intent over the task with the sheen of sweat on her forehead and upper lip, hands sticky with fruit or vegetable juices, one bra strap escaping over her shoulder, and her flushed face framed by moist ringlets.

Occasionally her mother, Grandma Amelia, would arrive by the 6 a.m. bus to help.

She always brought bread dough she had mixed the night before to make doughboys and pizza with thick red slices of our ripe fresh tomatoes, basil, oregano, garlic, and cheese sprinkled on bubbly dough and baked on Mom's old seasoned pizza pans. The aroma filled the house by 7 when we came down from bed. We could have a hot doughboy sprinkled with sugar and a piece of pizza for breakfast, she said with a wink. But, the spoonful of cod liver oil that always followed breakfast spoiled it. Making sure you did not gag was important as even a little dribble on your clothes would smell nasty all day. It would also reappear with a vengeance when the hot iron hit a freshly laundered blouse even weeks later.

Mom was already humming at her work and didn't seem to mind the sweat beaded on her face when mason jars were sterilized, pots steamed, and all of us were at work. It was her war factory geared to feed her little army. The ice cream man's bell announced break time, and she joined us on the front steps for some relatively cool fresh air.

Her mother, Amelia, was the only grandparent we knew. Her Dad, Antonio, was a barber and died prematurely. Eve and Ori remembered Dad's father, but we younger ones didn't. His name was Caesar, an imposing presence and a chemist, and Dad's mother,

Nicholetta, brought their family to America when Dad was seven years old from a town on the Adriatic near Chiete east of Rome. He spoke no English but did well in public school and was accepted at age 17 into Brown University. Grandma Amelia gave us sewing machine, crocheting, and embroidery lessons. She'd pinch your arm or poke you with a needle if you made too many mistakes and in frustration sputter, "Ooh fah! That's not the way I showed you!" She was tough but pretty with penetrating light opalescent blue eyes that could be frightening.

Chapter 4

Today, too soon for canning, we had the 50 x 100 ft. yard minus the house, garden, and garage footprints to use in making up ways to entertain ourselves. Sometimes we could go beyond the white picket fence and use the sidewalk. It felt like a trip to the beach. "Occupy your sisters", "Stay in the yard", "Who's crying", "Don't make me come out there" would be heard often today. My least favorite shouts were "Share and share alike" and "No! No friends in the yard. That's why I gave you sisters". The former really meant that no one owned anything exclusively in this house, and the latter that no outsiders could come to help relieve the tedium.

Neighborhood friends, peddlers, the morning and afternoon mail and newspaper editions deliveries, and our many delivery men would say hello to the three, soon to be four, little girls with their feet on the bottom rung of the fence. The sidewalk was wide enough for hopscotch and added a nice sharp turn to the driveway for our bikes when we were allowed to use it. Buddy, our next door neighbor's beagle, stayed with us all day. Sometimes we played dress up by making wedgy high heels that were currently in vogue out of the wood left from shaping the stakes and tying them to our bare feet with string—instant wedge high heals and splinters. There were several other children who received permission sometimes to come in the yard. Walter, Sheila, Anthony, and the Meyers girls could stay until lunch or someone caused a ruckus, and Mom sent them all home.

Our name is Cipolla which means onion in Italian. Dad called us his "patch of little rareripes." Our house was on Sandringham Avenue, our phone number was Plantations 5559, a two party line at first. We were instructed carefully in the etiquette and deference due our anonymous partner in this arrangement. The street had a gentle hill a block from our house that was great for sledding in the winter, and the boys roller skated and raced their bikes on it in the summer. Off limits naturally to us, we were happy spectators from our fence perch for the ruffians. The house was a cottage with separate garage built in 1936 by our Godfather, Anthony Mattromalo. It had four rooms and a bath on the first floor and two large rooms and an unfinished bath on the second.

The kitchen had cream-marbled-with-green

linoleum and cream walls above green stained wainscoting and paneling, with cabinets and moulding stained to match. The kitchen table and chairs were of blond wood with an art deco shaped chair back and detail in green on the splat. The table top was cream enamel bordered in green with a larger version of the chair's green detail. It opened to accommodate all of us and a few guests.

But best of all was what invitingly occupied the full length of the street across from us. Sandringham Avenue forms the northern border of impressive Providence College - lush with trees and beautifully landscaped. Construction was under way there directly across from our house. Later it became the athletic complex, but now there was a low building and parade ground for ROTC students at the construction point farthest from our street. Mostly it was just slowly being filled and leveled with boulders, clean waste, and landscaping refuse. It too was off limits. But sometimes when cousins came to visit or Mom was outside, we were allowed to play there. The rocks made great hiding places, make believe forts, houses, stores, boats, towers, or whatever we could dream up. A lot of explaining was necessary before any of these fantasies got up and running. Someone always cried. There were little green snakes among the rocks. You could get everyone back in the yard quickly by screaming, "Snake!"

The sprinkler was available if we were desperate. For winter play, the cellar had a kitchen, Dad's office rooms, but the boiler room was where we roller skated and played school. It was another scary place with its large white, many-armed boiler. Dad's and another man's initials and a date had been inscribed on it, and it was frightening when it fired up. I thought it fun to shut the light off on my sisters and run upstairs. Their panicked scramble and screams were worth Mom's scolding. I wanted to be good, but it was hard sometimes.

I flunked kindergarten, my first and only day of it last September. Dad rescued me after waiting an hour at the school's entrance where he could hear me crying. The smell and sounds of the place and the stern women in Cuban heels and dark crepe dresses were not for me. I was too young, it was determined. I would start in the first grade at St. Pius School with the Dominican nuns in the fall and could walk there with Eve and Ori. It would be fine. It was on the other side of the Providence College campus, and I loved the journey through it and its wonderland display for each season. The smell and rustle of leaves under foot of fall, the crunch of snow and steam rising from the roofs of busy brick buildings in winter, and the magic of spring's flowers and bird call were offered us in copious portions.

Chapter 5

The closest structure on the campus to our house was a white Dutch colonial house. It was on our route to and from school. Some of the friars shared this well kept ordinary house with beautiful flower and vegetable gardens. P.C.'s athletic program had selected the Dalmatian as the college teams' mascot and kept the two dogs at this house. Hence the house was dubbed "The Dog House". We would pass it quietly.

Evelyn and Orietta were timid with dogs and anxiously related their encounter with the Friars' two Dalmatians that chased them one day from that house while crossing the campus on their way home from school. They were saved by Father Sherer who heard their shrieks from his room and dashed out to scold the dogs off.

That's how we met and he joined our family, rushing from this house on a little mission of caring and mercy like those he would repeat many times for many, many years and for many people.

I loved dogs if they were friendly. The best thing about these two dogs was that they wore the same black and white colors as their owners. Much was black and white at that time with not a tinge of gray to anything. Even the adults lived by a rigid right-is-right creed that is still valid. Everything else was "Nonsense", Dad's favorite word.

The Friars were impressive. They wore a white habit with a black belt, a long straight scapular piece in front and back, and a hooded cowl. Their black trousers, shiny shoes, and black socks would show when they sat down on the curb to talk with us or take a turn with jacks or hopscotch. In winter they wore a long black cape like a tent. When the wind blew it billowed, and they looked as if they could fly. Each day the Friars read their required daily Office prayers. Many of them combined this with a walk around the perimeter of the campus. It must have been welcome fresh air and exercise after hours on end in classrooms filled with young men. These were Dominican Friars and used the designation O.P. after their names. Order of Preachers describes their vocation. They take vows of poverty, chastity, and obedience as do the Dominican Sisters. They were the essence of cleanliness, intelligence, and serenity to us, and the personification of honesty and reverence. There were many of them in our lives. Our church pastor, Father Conaty, was a caring and close friend to us all, but we saw him only at school or church. Fr. Brennan and Dad were casual friends.

Providence College was chartered in 1908 when Providence's Bishop Harkins asked the Dominican Friars of the Province of St. Joseph Order to establish a college in Providence. A parcel of seventeen acres on the north side of the city was purchased with donations from many local people. Pope Benedict and the R. I. General Assembly consented.

It was created as a center of advanced learning open to students of all faiths and peoples advising that "No person shall be refused admission." Bishop Harkins Hall was dedicated in 1917 and opened its doors to a class of seventeen male students and nine Dominican faculty. Guzman Hall, residence for Dominican pre-ecclesiastical students opened in 1926, and in 1929, the college purchased Thomas Hall or "The Dog House". In 1933 the college awarded its first Ph.D. degree. Aquinas Hall was built in 1939.

At that time the campus was comprised of Harkins Hall, Aquinas Hall, Guzman Hall, Thomas Hall, an ROTC center, and the Grotto.

The balance of campus was lovely grassy grounds with paved paths. It was a humble start to today's 50 plus buildings on 56 acres with more expansion planned.

We watched quietly as the priests would pass the house. Nearly always, they would nod to us or say hello. Sometimes one would stop and sit on the curb or join our games. One of them liked hopscotch and was funny to watch as he laughed and jumped. They would always leave with a gestured blessing over us. We liked them.

Mom knew some of them from church where they helped Father Conaty at our Dominican St. Pius Church and school. She joined the Dominican Tertiary Order for the laity which met at the college. As such, she was allowed to wear the habit of the Dominican Sisters at burial, which she did. One of their Friar mentors was Father Sherer who would bring Communion to her when she was ill. He was the Friar who flew with habit floating behind him to rescue my sisters from the dogs. I have a special love for Dalmatians for bringing him to us.

He had stopped by at other times and always talked with us, mostly about sanctity. He gave us small prayers to say as many times as we could each day to remind us that Jesus was always

Aerial view of Providence College — 1939
The Dog House appears on far left just above
center.

with us and loved us. Then the next time we saw him, he would ask how many times we repeated them. "Hundreds, at least!", we tried to outdo one another. Sometimes, there were Oh Henry candy bars for all. But he would suggest that we not eat the candy until the next day to learn self-discipline and control, and he would remember to check asking to see the candy. Someone always cried.

Rev. Joseph M. Sherer, or Father Joe, as some called him, was a tall, broad-shouldered German American and 43 years of age. He was raised in Ohio, in a loving, comfortable family of eight children, and was a professor of philosophy and chemistry at the College. His deep raspy voice, blue eyes that twinkled behind his glasses, and the rich laugh we heard often promised friendship, trust, and playfulness. He was a hit with us from the start. He carried himself with the dignity and strength of a representative of God, a priest. He was all goodness and kindness. Upright character and strength defined him. He would easily tear up in compassion if someone was hurt or sad. One of us would see him approaching the house and announce excitedly, "Father's here!" We cleaned his glasses, and grabbed his hand to show him our report cards or new toys. We trusted his kindness and good will on a deep instinctive level. He didn't campaign for it. Dad observed at a distance, his ambivalence toward religiosity evident.

Certainly as devout as any of the other Friars, he enjoyed with rare permission a diversion. Of these, fishing was high on his list as were good cigars and brandy. We smelled his cognac dipped cigars before we saw him. He tried to discuss fishing with Dad and offered him both of the other rare luxuries. Dad wasn't interested. There was tension in Dad's bearing when Father was around. Father's playful zest for life banged against Dad's quieter, reserved, often wary demeanor. Father generously offered science-laced advice on practical household problems that set Dad's check twitching. Not a good thing. Dad was usually at home all day working at his drafting table but did not spend much time after a brief hello with Father.

He was not impressed by appearances or symbols of rank or authority, and Father certainly bore many. Dad would reserve judgment about this man. Father was a complicated issue. He expressed his impatience with this ever-increasing, larger-than-life presence in the privacy of his home to Mom.

"Priests belong in church", and "I don't like him bouncing my children on his knee," I overheard him say. "Isn't he supposed to be impoverished," evoked a stern reproach from Mom that those treats were gifts from his caring mother in Ohio. He had neither car nor money and could not own anything. He received a small allowance from the Order with which he bought rosaries and prayer books for those in need.

"His work is to be with the people to help and preach", she continued. "He's a man of God who is a good, generous, and warm person who misses the fellowship of his family. It is wrong to deny friendship to anyone, especially a servant of God."

I think Dad felt it shouldn't be our family that provided it. He revealed the reason for his feelings by flatly saying, "A priest is still a man." Mom thought he had just made her argument.

A family three blocks away also had the company of another Friar who would be invited to dinner regularly and had the same impact on that family and the same reaction from the man of the house.

Father joined our dinner table a couple of times a month. Dad was never very interested in food. If Mom asked what he would like to have for dinner, his response would be that we all talk too much about food. He was happiest with a simple egg omelet. We learned how to make another of his favorites by cracking an egg in a small bowl and whipping it frothy before adding a half cup milk, some coffee or vanilla extract, and two tablespoons of sugar and whipping that all together into a delicious eggnog.

He spent little time at the table and finished his dinner quickly when Father was there, with his work waiting downstairs. Sympathetic and generous, Father would find ways to try to help. He often insisted on doing the dishes which meant four or five of us at the job as he explained the chemistry and types of nasty creatures that could lurk in the dish cloth and towels, the composition of soap, and the benefits of air drying the dishes. He enjoyed our conversation and teasing.

He shouldn't have been so helpful as it made everything worse. If a light bulb had blown or a faucet leaked, he would arrive the next day with a bulb, washer, and wrench. Dad finally stopped objecting. Father was now the family handyman as well as spiritual minister.

Round-up in R.I. of German and Italian aliens
believed to be dangerous to the safety of the nation was
underway early this morning. The FBI refused to make known
how many non-citizens of German or Italian extraction are
under suspicion or to say whether those taken in the state-
wide dragnet would be detained other than for questioning.
The Providence Journal, 12/9/1949

Chapter 6

Temporal matters were not Father's realm nor real concern, but he would wholeheartedly apply himself to them if it was needed. Spiritual health was primary, and he settled in as our personal family priest. During times of war a priest could hear men's confessions at any place, and Dad and his crew became a mission. He left one of his blessed scapulars in the drawer of a living room end table for this devout purpose. It was purple and white satin embroidered with Latin letters. It was narrow, and he kissed a little embroidered red cross on the back of it before draping it around his neck.

He did not hear Dad's confession, but I think a few of the men might have received the sacrament. Dad's beliefs were his affair. He didn't want to talk about them, but he lived by them. Although not voiced, telling another man intimate feelings and actions even in Confession was improper to him. He didn't need it. Father knew how Dad felt and sensitively avoided the subject with him and respected him for it. He didn't need help. I had the impression that Dad might have thought all this praying was for women. Mom considered it all an amazing blessing. Father would help protect her family from harm and guide our spiritual journey.

Our parents' feelings aside, we were delighted with this new pal. Always willing to play a game or help with a project, his time with us was a noisy combination of our vying for his attention and our mirth mixed with his rolling laughter. He always removed his Roman collar and black vest when he came.

Dad was not so pleased, but acquiesced. He was cordial and respectful but had very strong feelings about propriety and privacy. He was not to be dissuaded. This had the feeling of an invasion of his home, and he might become the outsider.

Mom had established a routine where we all knelt to say a rosary in the living room, and a sort of pray together, stay together nightly routine began. Dad joined us some times as did Father when he was there. He appreciated and felt the goodness of all his children and Mom in prayer together around him before bed. We began to sense that he was slowly coming to respect and accept Father as a friend and man. Father showed a deep love for us all, including Dad. We knew he was bringing this devotion and his presence to other families in the area also.

Once they got to know each other well and had developed the boundaries any deferential relationship has, all was better. Father learned what sort of humor elicited a laugh from Dad, and they enjoyed things that were too adult for our little heads. They got along better. But to me, Dad seemed to include little of the warmth in his contact with Father that was evident in his other relationships. They did have long conversations about the meaning of life and common sense component of activities, government, and industry. There was an intellectual parity built of differing experiences and backgrounds that appealed to both. I wonder if they may have discussed that they both had ancestral roots in two of the Axis nations. But, secure in their love of this country, I don't think it was an issue in any way in their lives. Father once brought a young man in a colorful military uniform to meet Dad. I don't know what army or organization his outfit represented, it looked Austrian or Prussian, perhaps. He was regaled like the prince at Cinderella's ball or one of the dancing toy soldiers. Father was proud of the young student who was a relation from Ohio.

The war raged on. Father's contribution to Mom's preserve cellar was to be home brewed root beer for us and real beer for Dad. Mom was pleased. We were excited. It would be a neat chemical experiment, he said. Soon he brought a large new crock to fill with sassafras, hops, yeast, sugar, and printed recipes for the root beer which we thought he wouldn't need. We all pitched in boiling the fragrant concoctions and filling the crock. A spot in the furnace room was selected for fermentation, and gauze was tied over the top. He explained each ingredient and step along the way. We checked it daily. During the first couple of days nothing happened. Then some foam appeared, then a lot of dirty looking foam. He said it should ferment for five or six days. It did. The drink was golden brown and fizzy. It was good!

Then he brought bottles and a length of red rubber siphoning tube which he showed us how to use to fill a dozen or so of them. He brought a bottle cap machine with a lever you forced down to crimp the cap tightly in place. That added another dimension to Mom's larder. Dad didn't seem to care. We were fascinated by the process and clamored around him trying not to miss a thing. He answered all our questions patiently and mediated the "it's my turn" issues. We darted about getting things he needed.

Buoyed by this success, he started on home-brewed beer. We repeated the process this time using sticky malt in cans, hops in cans with beautiful labels, yeast, and sugar. The same white crock and gauze were employed in the same place. This brew's fermenting time was about two weeks. The bottling was fun. It was added to the preserve cellar.

However, after a few days, the bottles started exploding, mostly at night. This did get Dad to care. It must have sounded like a gun shot beneath his bed. He was jolted awake. We could hear it on the second floor followed by his expletives and scrambling about. Somehow, Father was able to resolve this, and things settled down. Dad grumbled to Mom that for what it had cost for all the ingredients and equipment, we could have bought Father several cases of good beer. He didn't like the taste of Father's brew. Dad's patience was being tested. I think Father sensed it also, but not much changed. We girls cleaned up the mess.

The 10 cent beer is gone as
wholesale costs increase
18 to 20 cents per case of 24 bottles.
September 1953

Chapter 7

My sharpest memory of WWII occurred one summer night. As required, we had blacked out with dark paper and tape the cellar windows where Dad worked at night. At about 8 o'clock the air raid warning sirens wailed scaring everyone. It was a drill, and we were to shut off all the lights. Then we were to look for airplanes, maybe. We ran through the house to be sure no lights were on and gathered on the front steps to listen for aircraft and trade comforting words with neighbors also huddled on alert. The night was charged with excitement and fear. It was warm and clear. Dad continued to work in the cellar with his one drafting table lamp on.

After about 30 minutes, a white helmeted man with a night stick on his belt came into the yard and demanded that we shut off the lights in the cellar. We were violating a federal law punishable by fines or even arrest, and he had the legal responsibility to enforce it. Hearing the commotion, Dad appeared. He was soundly scolded by the warden and threatened with arrest. Dad had heard the gruff manner in which the warden spoke to Mom. Something in the man's posture, words, or maybe he was known to Dad triggered a very angry response. It seems the light from the cellar was a tiny sliver along the top edge of a small cellar window where the tape had failed to adhere properly. The warden obviously enjoyed his role and played it to maximum fearsomeness for all within earshot.

I think that's what most incensed Daddy. This man was posturing, being a showoff, silly, and extremely puffed up by his position. Dad shouted something like just try arresting or fining me. We had run downstairs in the meantime and fixed the offending window although from the inside it wasn't evident. The episode ended with Dad asking this "poppinjay" who would feed his family if he couldn't work at night. His evident lack of respect and what at the time should have been a combination of fear and American loyal submission seemed to take the steam out of the man, and he left. It was a terrifying event for us children and brought us to our knees with Mom to pray for everyone's safety and especially for those families like ours in Europe hearing real planes and bombs.

This was the first time I saw how Daddy's quiet demeanor masked an awful intensity if provoked. I would see it again. As the pressures of his work and family needs grew, he carried more and more unrelieved stress. It made him seem unhappy and angry.

SERVICEMEN'S
PROVIDENCE JOURNAL CANTEEN CLOSES
Operated from December 29, 1943, to December 24, 1945,
with local women as "Junior Hostesses", canteen closes.
1945

Chapter 8

One afternoon when the field crews returned and were making their reports in the driveway, Dad spotted Father approaching from down the street. This end of workday ritual was a high-spirited reunion for him. He wanted to hear the day's successes and reveled in stories of their funny situations. It was an upbeat break in his day. Father would end that exchange. Dad saw him approaching from a block away, and lowering his voice with obvious annoyance said, "Damn it! Here comes Father Schnapps." I didn't know what a schnapp was but knew it was an insult. I felt sorry for Father. There was a muffled laugh from everyone, and instantly Dad seemed to regret saying it. Too late, the sobriquet stuck. He would scowl when someone else used it later. It was not like him to criticize or poke fun behind one's back. Always the champion of the underdog, he felt protective now and contrite. However, he too would let it slip later with wry humor. I'm sure he had some more salty words he suppressed instead.

Although Dad was often torn in how to deal with Father, we continued in this pleasant way. Father was there for any of us who might need anything he could provide. His moral strength and sincere generosity and goodness were always evident. He and Father had pleasant talks when Dad had a moment. These gradually became more frequent. I wonder what topics they discussed, and am sure it was not religion or Dad's piety. There was a good deal of laughter probably generated from the wry sense of humor they both had and their feel for irony. But Father always had time for anyone of us to sit and listen to anything we wanted to share with him. He would respond seriously and warmly on any issue.

We got a television set in 1948. Instantly captivated as was the rest of America, we watched in awe. We were fascinated by the range and behavior of people in other places. Everyone was so happy and gay. We saw talent, sophistication, elegance, violence, and a world so vast as to astound.

During Friday night Gillette fights from Madison Square Garden, a card game was held at least once a month and was Dad's only recreation that I can recall. Three or four male friends or family members would come and sit around the card table. We all helped quietly to get glasses, snacks, sandwiches, and drinks. Ash trays always needed emptying. Mom stayed in other rooms.

One of these nights, Father dropped by dressed more formally in his black suit and roman collar. I don't know if Mom had invited him. He accepted a beer and started chatting with the men. After a while he quietly left the living room, and one of the men followed him down cellar. I saw him retrieve his scapular from the table drawer. No one else seemed to notice except Dad. When they returned, everything continued as normal, and Father joined them in a beer before leaving.

However, when everyone else had left, we heard Mom and Dad arguing. Father had stepped over the line this time. I think Dad was as much astounded as incensed. I found out later that Mom had urged her brother who was recently divorced to talk confidentially to Father. He would never have refused. If someone needed him, Father was available wherever and whenever, even if it incurred Dad's displeasure. Mom could find no real fault. What could be done? They went to bed. However, it became another source of teasing among the men when they saw Father. Guesses as to who among them should be careful because of some shared knowledge, and who needed Confession most was the gist of a good deal of ribbing.

Rev. Joseph M. Sherer, O.P.

Chapter 9

For so large a family in a small cottage it was surprisingly peaceful, but there were occasional mishaps which unsettled everything. Regrettably, a good many of them swirled about me. In 1947 we finally had a brother, and Mom and Dad a son. Jane was no longer the baby. He was Peter also and everyone loved and doted on him. There was much excitement from extended family and Father about his arrival. Why all the fuss? Another baby. Now we were seven. Jane joined me in my bed upstairs, and infant Peter went into the same crib she had occupied in Mom and Dad's room. We used the same diapers and pail, the same bottles and sterilizer pan, and the same crib and carriage. However, he got new blue clothing and toys for a boy.

For Mom this pregnancy also had complications, and he was delivered caesarian section. He came home before Mom did. His care was a group effort by Evelyn and Ori primarily when they were at home. When Mom returned she was confined to her bed for a very long time. I had more time at home and was permitted to provide much of Peter's daily needs. He was very cute and very happy. No trouble ever.

Mom's doctor, Hugh Hall, who delivered all of us, would visit the house every Saturday unless needed before that. He arrived in a long light blue Cadillac often with the top down. He wore a white linen blazer with tan trousers and a bow tie, and sported a neat white mustache.

Dr. Hall smoked cigars and would take a glass of wine with Dad before he left. Anyone with sniffles or a complaint would be seen, but Mom was his concern. She got shots and prescriptions. The three of them seemed to enjoy these visits which were conducted leisurely. We girls would take turns carrying his interesting black bag. The baby was thriving. We listened at their feet and fetched anything they needed.

Besides changing and washing diapers, I would prepare bottles and feed and bathe him, as did we all. He was a wonder to us in many ways. The real thing after all the playing dolls and house in the cellar.

Mom liked us to get the sun when possible, and 10-month old Peter needed airing too. I took him often in the carriage along the sidewalk and driveway. Mom praised my babysitting skills to friends, family, and to me often. How would it have been possible not to acquire that skill in our home for any of us. She said she depended on me and my sisters.

One warm day I was to walk the baby and asked if I could go two houses over to spend a few minutes with Sheila. She was a friend to all of us and was moving to California. Mom said I might but to be very careful and stay only a short time. It was a pleasant little walk. When we arrived, I picked up Peter and went into the house.

Sheila's mom sent us to the basement to play because they were packing to leave. There were piles of empty boxes all over the cellar. Sheila wanted to give me some trading cards, both the bubble gum pack and paired playing card types. She also wanted to show me some pretty marbles she had gotten. I looked around for some way to safely put Peter down and spotted the perfect empty box. It was round with a smooth metal rim about a yard in diameter and only a foot deep. I sat him in the middle of it, a perfect make-believe play pen. He happily took his toy in his chubby fingers. I sat on the concrete floor next to him.

We stayed about 10 minutes, and then it was time to leave. I reached over to pick up my playful little brother and froze. His arms and legs, clothes, and face were as blue as the sky. Sheila was speechless also. I wrapped my arms around him and ran out of the house dodging her mother. When I got home, I put him in the playpen in the back porch, got a soapy face cloth and towel. I took off all his clothes and hid them under the couch to deal with later. Then I tried to remove the blue color. He got bluer. He was as jolly as always and chuckled as though my efforts to de-color him were playful tickling. The creases in his thighs and under his neck were like white bracelets. There was no denying that this was very serious. He could be permanently harmed, and I had done it. I would be killed or sent away for this. I wanted Father to show up, but he didn't. Dad was in his office. Mom was in the kitchen. There was nothing else for me to do, I had to get him help and face the music.

As I expected, there was stunned silence at first and then a deep moaning sound that grew in volume when Mom saw her only son. Dad arrived at a run. We must have been a sight, my blue baby brother and me ghostly white except for my hands and cheeks where I had cuddled him. He was neon blue now, and I was colorless. In their concerned fussing over him, I moved out of the center of it and watched. They calmed down when they saw how well he was even if he didn't look it. Dad called Dr. Hall who would be right over.

Then that awful controlled, slowly articulated questioning began. I was picked up by my upper arms to stand on a chair stiff with fear. With their faces very close to mine, I was asked to give a minute by minute recital of everything I did from leaving home until returning. When I had barely finished Dad ran to Sheila's and returned with the box she told him Peter had been in. It was the right one.

He grabbed the phone again and read the label to someone, the pharmacist maybe, explaining what happened. Shockingly, he laughed a little and hung up. He came to me and squeezed my hand in his usual way. I tried to force down the huge lump in my throat. After a calming talk with Mom and the arrival of Dr. Hall, Peter was given a lengthy bath, lots of baby oil, and clean clothes. He would be just fine in a few days. The box had contained a harmless type of laundry bluing powder. The baby had not ingested any of it and showed no allergic or irritation reactions. It would be completely gone in no time. I got a little hug from the doctor.

Not soon enough though for a sickly silence to follow me for days. I was deeply shaken. Dad and Mom seemed to have forgiven me, but I wondered how much stature I had lost. My sisters looked silently at me with serious faces and large eyes. Father just tsk-tsk'ed a few times and reassured them that the compound was harmless. I felt like an elephant in the room and too noisy if I had to speak. There was nowhere to go, and I wanted a dark corner to hide in. But eventually, it was forgotten, and I had my place in the family back. There were always ways to reconfirm one's value to the family.

Chapter 10

Father arrived one day in tan trousers and a plaid shirt, looking very unusual and strange without the Roman collar. He was driving the college's small car which was for use by the Friars. This day he was going fishing for a couple of hours and said he would bring us anything he caught. We helped him dig in the garden for worms after he showed us how to wet an area and wait. I begged to go with him. Mom hesitated a moment and then agreed. Father had a variety of rods and reels in the car.

We drove to a pond with a factory on one side and homes all around the rest. He parked the car on the street nearby, and we toted the gear along a rough path. The pond was dark blue and sparkled with the light breeze. There was a convenient log dragged to the water's edge that had initials   carved into it and looked like a favorite spot for neighborhood wading and picnicking. A lovely old maple tree hung low over it all.

As it was just a short distance by car from the college, Father had fished here before and described our quarry. Horn Pout it was called. He told me about his dear friend in Swansea who fished with him. He showed me the colorful large lures used for salt water fishing and what fish they were designed to attract. He showed me how to prepare the line. He helped put the reluctant worms on the hook. Eager monkey that I was, I had no trouble learning how to cast after he showed how it was done with a couple of whizzing arcs through the air that landed near the center of the small pond. That was all it took! We settled down.

It was peaceful and enjoyable to sit on the log and wait for a bite. The sun was high, and it was warm. Father smoked his pipe and smiled contentedly. Whenever we had a few moments alone with him, some religious sermonizing would begin. I expected it and waited quietly. In his tackle box were a chilled coke, cookies, and a candy bar the housekeeper packed for his excursion. He said she didn't like fish. He took the cap off the coke, gave it to me, and handed me an Oh Henry bar. What a treat! I imagined how wonderful to be grown up and free to go about enjoying the sun, water, anything, and anywhere I wanted. Then he started by marveling briefly at God's goodness in nature's bounty around us (which was obvious at this moment even to me).

"Do you see His hand in everything and thank him for these blessings? If you see your life and the world this way you cannot be unhappy or lonely." He said with the pipe between his teeth.

"I don't want to hurt the fish", I ventured. "Won't God be mad?"

"Not if we are humane and not wasteful. You know that, don't you? We help keep God's design and balance also. Human needs are important also. We give Him praise by using His gifts wisely and thanking Him for all He has given us as we humbly accept them. We must always guard against the sin of pride."

"What if I'm proud of my report card. Is that being not humble? Can you be humble and proud at the same time," I said to seem interested and a bit to disturb his train of thought, I guess, but didn't really know what I was asking or wanting an answer. I was just playing with words to match his.

"Humm. That's a good question", he answered. "We shouldn't take pride in things that are gifts from God; and instead of being proud you can be grateful to God for helping you to use them. Do you understand?"

"Oh fudge!" Enough. Can't we just fish?" I thought.

"You should help your sisters and friends by your example to love and see Him also, to appreciate every moment with joy as His gift. Do you think you can?"

"Yes, Father, I'll try."

"Well, good for you. Jesus sees you trying and knows you're not selfish. Selfishness is unhealthy for body and soul. Learn of the sacrifices and self-discipline of the great saints. I'll bring you a book on their lives."

"Yes, yes, yes," I thought but said, "Thank you". He had said all this before. He was spoiling everything. Maybe someone told him something? I quickly examined my conscience. I could be selfish at times and mean. He did bring that book some years later as a grammar school graduation gift. We had all learned to try to avoid little holy talks.

"I hate squash," sweet Mariann said once which provoked a talk to us all on the philosophical aspect of hate, its dark, corrosive, spirit deadening abilities, and the presence of God in love, its opposite.

But that was it, no more than a long minute. No more holy talk. He didn't want to spoil this rare pleasure either. He rambled on about the dock at his friend's house in Swansea and the type of boat they used, and how they dug for quahogs and steamer clams at low tide. He described how they cooked the fish in his home and had dinner together. He seemed to have enjoyed these outings with that friend greatly and the telling was as good.

We got a bite. The red and white bobber disappeared then came back up. I squealed and yanked. He patiently showed me how to reel it in. It fought for its freedom flopping about on the ground. How brutal, but I felt sad and excited. It had horns! Ugly, greenish, and slimy were my first impressions, but it was thrilling to have gotten one. It was about 8 inches long and nothing like what the fish monger had on ice in his truck each Friday. I caught the next two and Father three more. He put them in a pail with some water, and we proudly brought them home. In the cellar kitchen, Father cleaned them, and we prepared the pan. We fried them after dredging in cornmeal as he instructed and shared with anyone who wanted some. Father ate the fish. He was very happy. I had some. It was delicious. We were not raised with menu choices at meals. What Mom served we ate and liked. We all liked Horn Pout now.

Dad arrived home about that time and declined some fish but stayed a few minutes with us to have a drink and quick chat with Father. He saw I was excited, and with little coaching I rattled off my experience.

"Father took me fishing. I caught three fish. I know how to fish now, Dad. Father let me use a fishing pole. You have to watch a red thing, and it moves if a fish is nibbling at the bait, and you have to yank it up. There must be hundreds of fish in that pond. We caught all of these in just a little time. It was wonderful."

Somewhere around the fourth "fish" reference, I could see that he was not happy. His cheek twitched, and he squinted slightly. He went upstairs, and I heard him and Mom in some quick exchanges. Then silence. This was definitely something that did not meet Dad's code of something and must be "nonsense", but he didn't say or do anything about it. I knew I had disappointed him. Through mixed emotions, I tried to understand. Here were two wonderful men. They were very important to us all. Did I ruin everything again? Was being a girl at the heart of it? Daddy knew of the perils ahead for his brood of vulnerable daughters but wanted to shield us for as long as he could. But, this was Father Sherer.

Nothing changed. Father came as usual. We welcomed him with glee. Dad was cordial and buried himself in his work. He had no choice.

His business was growing with the returning troops now that the war was over.

I hope he never felt we could favor Father over him.

Chapter 11

But so were we growing, and now filled that little house. It was harder to keep us out of each other's hair. One evening at dinner in the basement kitchen Ori had had enough of my pesky teasing and as she called it, my insolence! I was always in her way, it seemed. I did like to tease her with the dogs she feared, but slurping my soup (deliberately) when she said to "Stop It!" was the limit. She lifted her dish of beans and pasta and broke it over my head. I was stunned but continued stubbornly to eat my meal noisily but with all other proper etiquette and gentility, my only defense.

She liked to tell this story whenever we were reminiscing and comment that she often laughed at the memory of noodles covering my hair and dripping down my face as I tried to appear not to notice, and I joined her in that. Sisters will tell you frankly things about yourself that others would never dare to say.

It's a funny memory of life in that little house. Luckily the folks were not with us, and no one told them about it. The younger ones watched with shocked wide eyes.

Mayhem visited us at times. It rushes at you like a shroud of bats from a cave, dark and dangerous. A vividly remembered example happened on an innocent walk home with two pack members from my Girl Scout meeting. Mom and Dad had given me a great gift by allowing me to join the after school troupe. Our leader, Miss Lowe (yes, the same surname as the founder of the scouts, Juliet Lowe) was pretty, fun, and engaged to be married. Grandma's lessons with the needle, my child care and cooking with Mom helped in earning my badges. I loved it.

This day in spring, Joan and Sally were to come home with me to work on a scouting project and wait to be picked up by their parents. I knew Mom was baking a warm fragrant ginger bread she would top with whipped cream as a snack for us. My sisters would join in.

We crossed from the school to the Providence College campus and made a visit to its lovely stone grotto. From there we followed a walkway that lead to the back of Aquinas Hall instead of returning to the road that paralleled it. Joan and Sally had never seen this part of the campus and were drawn to lively sounds coming from the windows of the building's basement. We peered down on students enjoying the game tables and shouting rowdy exchanges.

One of them noticed us and set up a whoop. In a flash they ran from the room, and we shrieked and took off toward home. It seemed to me that they just wanted to scare us away from staring at them and that that was the end of it. Then I heard their heavy pounding footsteps round the corner of the building and bear down on us at full speed. Oh, dear God! Could I ever have a nightmare that was worse than this. They could easily catch us but didn't seem to be really trying. It was like the chase and our panic was their game and teenagers' sadistic prank. We screamed and ran as fast as we could. There was loud laughter and calls to stop from the boys.

"Don't go to my house!" I shouted as loudly as possible to Joan and Sally, but they were sobbing and didn't hear me. We made it ahead of the boys, and Nancy and Sally pounded on the front door yelling.

"Mr. Cipolla, help, help, help! Please Help!" I tried to get them to calm down and stop screaming. I knew the boys wouldn't follow us into our yard, and I didn't want Dad involved. Too late. Within minutes the door swung open to reveal Dad in his rolled up shirt sleeves and a shocked look on his face. He looked ten feet tall. Nancy blubbered the situation and pointed to the boys who were now walking down a side street enjoying their escapade. Dad's eyes squinted, his cheek twitched, and he took off after them calling for them to stop. They didn't. Instead they started to run again with Dad in pursuit. Mom settled us down to our snacks and project.

An hour or so later Dad returned. He asked how we were and said not to worry. We were safe and in no trouble, and that it would not happen again. He warned us not to walk near the buildings. All was fine. I wasn't told I could no longer be a scout, and I never heard a word more about it. Was I really absolved of any blame for this unusual and horrendous occurrence? I couldn't believe it. We had been trespassing.

Dad explained to Mom when the girls had gone that he had had to chase those boys nearly the whole distance of the campus' perimeter. I would be the death of him! He followed them to a dorm, but went instead to the College President's office and demanded to see him. He asked to have Father Sherer contacted also. Both Dad and Father told the President that this behavior was neither worthy of the College nor could be tolerated in our neighborhood. With a clear description from Dad, the culprits were identified and expelled. I worry about them at times and pray they were able to overcome this harsh punishment. I deeply regret that they were involved in one of my predicaments.

Chapter 12

Big moments for us during the summer would be a ride after Dad returned from work to Rte. 6 in Massachusetts for foot long hot dogs. We'd each get one and a coke. I remember Dad asking for 25 cents worth of gasoline to get us home. Someone usually got car sick on that 40 minute ride. On more rare occasions, we would make it to the ocean for a day of surf, sun, and a picnic. How wonderful and exciting for us and a chance to see Mom and Dad lolling in a beach chair under an umbrella. Dad would roll his trousers up above his calves and wade with us at the waters edge. Mom stayed dry and tended the youngest who played at her side. The ride home was not so grand. The younger ones would sleep heavily against us or on our laps. Sunburn and beach sand added to the oven-like feeling of the backseat with its jumble of irritated legs, and wasn't fun. Traffic was usually slow, but mercifully Dad would stop half way home for ice cream cones for each of us. We would all pile out to stand in line and receive our cool treat. Mom always commented on how good the sun and sea were for us and how well we looked with our tans that would make the winter easier to bear.

With this in mind, the following summer Dad built a beach house for us. Our summers would be spent at the shore in the Pt. Judith section of Narragansett away from the confinement and dangers of city streets. Mom and the little ones (me down) moved there when school ended. It was a wonderful place. Dad, Ori, and Eve visited on weekends mostly.

Father came on the rare occasion that a car was available to him. We caught fiddler crabs for bait, and he fished a little before leaving. He gave me a tackle box, reel, and salt water pole which I kept under my bed in the middle room. It was stolen when the house was looted following hurricane Carol in 1954 and not replaced. After the storm we had not been allowed to drive past the center of Narragansett Pier to the house for days, affording many opportunities for thieves to go through the battered homes. We lost our front porch and its roof, but the cinderblock house survived. The waterline evident on the living room wall was above the fireplace mantle. Most of our neighbors' homes were completely obliterated with hardly any evidence that they had ever existed.

Dad and a friend, Tony, bought two oceanfront lots from our dentist for $500 each. Tony was a stone mason. Dad designed two identical cottages, surveyed the lots, and marked the foundations with batter boards and recorded the plans. Tony and Dad paid their crews to spend some time by the shore to dig the footings. Then Tony took over and constructed two identical cinderblock homes with a porch running the length of the ocean side.

There was to be a large beach stone fireplace in the living room. We used it nearly every day. The stones were to be a whitish, cantaloupe-size, and we were recruited to hunt for them along the shore. Tony rejected types that would crack from the heat. Dad and he selected the center keystone for over the hearth.

Three bedrooms, kitchen, bath, living room and porch were cozy enough for us. Mom was very happy there. Life was more manageable, and she had time to rest. Moving in was a logistical challenge. We had to load clothes, food, pillows, etc. into the car and all of us also. Once unloaded, a thorough cleaning was necessary. It was winter quarters to tiny field mice. The propane gas tanks were delivered and a balky water heater started. It blew out each time someone opened the kitchen door, was risky to start, and my job. The house had uncooperative metal casement windows. Someone would have to go out and push on them while another turned the reluctant handles and clamp locked them. The salt air was hard on everything except us. It was the closest any of us would ever come to camping. By the standards of the late 40's and to us, it was elegant.

Mom loved its coziness, but cozy felt like confinement to Dad. He enjoyed the realization that "there is only ocean between here and Europe". On clear nights he would take the transit out of the car's trunk and aim it at the stars. This awesome nature offered in the restless Atlantic Ocean and the sky before us silenced us as we looked and felt their influence. He knew the names of the constellations, and looking for the big and little dipper is something I still do. It was a way to be part of all this awesomeness.

We kids took to the place like a fling of sandpipers. Born with cup-half-full perspectives and bred can-do, it suited us perfectly. Days were spent picking mussels that mom would stuff with rice or bread dressing and steam for lunch on the beach.

The rocky shoreline teamed with fiddler crabs that we could catch and sell to Mr. Mason, the jovial, old toothless fisherman who lived across the street. He sold his fresh fish catch and quahogs to Mom who made chowder and clam cakes. TV reception was iffy so we played hours of gin rummy with Mom and applied lotion to each other's blistered faces, shoulders, and arms. We would often lose electrical power. The fireplace, gas stove, and hot water heater eliminated most of the real issues but left us playing cards and sipping hot chocolate while we read in the glow of firelight and candles.

Our popularity and destination appeal soared. Aunts in particular came often. It was good company but meant more work in the kitchen. They would drive up unexpectedly usually bearing a couple of dozen steaming clam cakes from the nearby lobster shack and pastries from the city. This meant they hoped to stay for dinner.

Mom sent us to Mr. Mason to buy three quarts of quahogs in the shell and whatever fresh fish he had. The aunts would join her in the kitchen to build a Rhode Island style clam chowder. This recipe makes a clear savory chowder whose flavor is uncompromised as with the other versions as it shuns both the heavy cream and the spicy tomato concoctions to offer a rich, flavorful soupier dish. The potatoes are cut into small wedges and allowed to over-cook a bit to thicken the broth.

Good and hearty on the beach with oyster crackers, especially for blue lipped kids who wouldn't get out of the water.

*Jane, Clare, Peter, Boots, and Mariann at the
beach house*

They would boil up sweet corn and bake the cod or haddock with a crispy topping and finish preparations with a green salad. If we could get crabs or lobsters and their husbands were there, a Fra Diavolo tomato sauce with cracked pieces of lobster and rich with lobster tamale and mild hot pepper (for the children) was served outside. The adults would add more crushed red pepper. Any of the children who whined about not wanting chowder for dinner could eat the salad and bread. No PBJ or pasta with butter was offered and they eventually joined in eating the family's fare.

Mom ruled that there was to be no changing in the bedrooms after swimming as wet bathing suits left on beds soaked through to her mattress. Always averse to uncomfortable dampness, her routine was to close and lock all the windows as soon as the sun was about to set. Dusk always brought a wet chilly breeze full of the Atlantic that beaded on the screens and made even flannel sheets clammy. Our rosy checks and healthy glow was what she and Dad had wanted for us. We all thrived there and had adventures that we recall happily in our get-togethers today.

Our neighbor Gracie had a Saint Bernard named Ricky. A very big, thick coated, slow moving, gentle dog. He was her baby, and she kept him by her at all times. Gracie would prepare a large pot of meat and vegetables for

Ricky each day. He had a huge appetite. Her son and daughter were out of college and working out of state but would visit occasionally. Otherwise, she depended on Mom for company and help when Tony, her husband, was away on a job. My bike was the only transportation we had at the beach. Neither woman drove. A trip to Adams' store about a mile from the house supplied emergency needs.

Father provided fishing poles and a tackle box, and we bought some hand lines. We were allowed to go to the cove to fish. This was a favorite spot for Mr. Mason and city people who drove to the area. To get there we had to go through a large area of cat tails taller than we were. I felt the only way to safely make it without coming upon a snake or something worse was to scream and make a run for it. Fun, that! Single file and screaming while we ran as fast as we could, we would manage the feat. Someone might have cried. We caught a large bass there once with a hand line and Mom baked it with a stuffing. It was very good.

After a heavy storm and surf, the pebbly beach would have long rows of seaweed left at the high water mark. A treasure hunt would begin for fishing lures mostly but also anything could be tangled in the seaweed. These we gave to Father or Mr. Mason and usually received some change for them. The run home was not so frantic. We had cut a path getting there, and we were all too exhausted to scream or run fast.

Our neighbor, Fred Mason, built a two room shanty with an outhouse many years before we arrived across the street from us for himself and his wife. They were from Connecticut, and I think this was a summer camp before he retired. It had a slightly canted flat roof and tar paper sides picturesquely covered with ivy. Inside it looked like a combination Asian hut and Arab tent. It had walls painted a pale blue then sponged with rows of silver and purple blossom-like shapes. Mrs. Mason's choice of decor included tented ceiling hangings of colorful lengths of fabric that were tacked to the middle of the ceiling and then draped from the top of the walls like a sheik's home. There were magazine photos tacked to the walls and beaded fringe on lamp shades. She was a large woman who wore floor length skirts and layered tops. Although we had never been to one, being inside her home was like a visit to an exotic circus performers tent. She was gentle and friendly.

Fred smiled toothlessly, laughed a good deal, and spent much time in his garden. Fish heads and seaweed were his choice of fertilizer. Each seed or small plant had this mix under its roots. The bane of his life was the numerous ground hogs that lived in the bushy areas around us. He mumbled and grumbled as he repaired and replaced the damaged garden each day. To trap the woodchucks, he anchored a lobster pot in the garden and baited it. To our horror, he didn't carry the trapped beasts to another location or even secretly drown them but killed them when we were close enough to see him spear them in the trap with the pointed metal rods he used to anchor the pots to the ocean floor.

It was bloody, brutal, and frightening. We told Dad. He was appalled and said Mr. Mason shouldn't have done that and added he couldn't understand what we had been thinking to stay and watch. He warned us not to be too friendly and to stay in the yard. Like in the city? Oh no! Although we did take his advice about being too friendly.

However, we were reminded soon thereafter of the brutality to animals some people are capable of when on July 4th all of our neighbors entertained large parties and strangers filled the beach lawn areas. During the festive afternoon, we noticed a noisy group of mostly adults gathering on the rocks that were slowly emerging from the ebbing tide in front of our house. They were shouting and laughing. Children were shrieking.

When we understood the cause of all the excitement we ran to rouse Dad from his rare day of rest in a lawn chair listening to a ballgame. He watched a moment, tensed, and approached the crowd of men who were lifting large stones and pounding a three foot long fish that looked like a juvenile sand shark. The hapless creature was stranded in a shallow pool amid the rocks.

"Stop!" Dad shouted to the men as he made his way on the slippery wet rocks in his leather shoes. They were unknown to us and looked him over, taking in his dress shoes, suit pants, and white shirt.

"Leave it alone!" he growled. They laughed to each other and continued raising large stones over their heads and trying to smash the fish.

"What the hell do you think you're doing." Dad shouted. "Go back home! This fish belongs here more than we do."

"Mind your own business", someone shouted, and the stoning continued.

Dad didn't answer but moved so he straddled the struggling shark, a foot on rocks each side of it. He had told us to remain at a distance, and we watched in terror as the crowd advanced on him. The grass areas along the beach were now filled with spectators shouting their opinions. He didn't move. Mom watched with her hands on her face and fear in her eyes. For a few moments it was a standoff and the men were quiet.

"If you want your kids swimming with sharks, you're nuts, Bub", someone shouted, but they slowly dropped their stones and started to leave. Dad bent down and grabbed the thrashing animal with two hands near its tail and lifted and dragged it the twenty or so yards to deeper water where it hurried into the surf.

No more was said. Everyone returned to their parties and dug into coolers, and their celebrations resumed. Mom said to stay off the beach until everyone went home. I looked at Dad who was back on his chair with his eyes shut against the sun and probably reality, and tried to process the incident. Was he fearless or just that appalled by the enjoyment those men had in the pain they administered. His outrage made a difference that day for the shark, and I smiled to myself as I felt again that rightness of it, and was warmed and very proud of him.

Fashion world embraces
tailored trouser suit over
ladies' dresses of prewar style.
December, 1941

Chapter 13

Despite the war, the 40's and 50's were decades swaddled in a haze of comfort and restlessness for us. Sheltered by Dad and Mom's solid conservatism based on common sense and an age old moral code, our home was sane and secure. Children were accepted in all their diversity and awkwardness. A docile group, we were very different from one another in temperament and interests. We grew up in a world of good or evil. Cruel and casual judgments were not flung about easily. Nerd, geek, hip, cool, etc. labels weren't in our vocabulary yet. Someone was good or bad and more casually nice or not nice based on their behavior. We were taught to recognize group think and urged not to cripple our minds by creating areas of thought which others had declared sensitive and banned. Often we were reminded to "Think for yourself". We couldn't hurt someone's feelings but that didn't mean crusading for every popular issue like sheep just to be considered one of the group. Father joined in with "our creativity and a free intellect were gifts of God and not to be surrendered to anyone".

The slippery slope of gray areas in moral behavior hadn't yet begun. Hollywood and some authors depicted teens as troubled due to their "more evolved, enlightened attitudes" on just about everything in American culture. This psychological perspective invaded our lives. We didn't know many rebels with or without a cause. Adults in our little world seemed not to notice whether or not a moral decline in American culture was happening. We were not exposed to it. Their steadiness anchored and protected us. Screaming bobby-sox'ers were in NY and CA. We thought them immature and goofy. Elvis was embarrassing, but we still enjoyed his music. Feelings, sensitivities, and understanding were required now of us all. It was confusing, annoying, and disruptive.

But we kept up. Cousin Connie taught us how to make poodle skirts with a felt appliqué by folding a yard of felt in half and with a pencil on a 36 inch string pinned in the center of the fold draw an arc line and cut on it. Then you shortened the string to 12 inches and cut the hole for the waist. We sewed elastic around the hole with a small slit placket and snap. A few minutes under a hot iron and the French Poodle appliqué was in place. Easy, easy! Connie was a display designer at Shepard's Department Store and quite a few years older than I. She was sweet, generous, and glamorous.

Our restlessness was a desire to share in the amazing new inventions whirling one after the other into existence. There was excitement in young people to try everything new, to fly places, to dream any dream. We could do anything. Dad and Mom's mantra continued to be that we were to be individuals, not to follow the crowd; that when you see everyone running to something, run the other way. All this new age stuff was "nonsense" and not to be allowed to derail us. We were to keep our feet on the ground. They were right, basically, and we complied.

I don't remember sit-downs ever with the parents to discuss how much they loved us or ask if we were happy or felt loved. We knew because they showed it; and when you needed that little bit more of loving comfort, it was provided in other ways. Mom would pat her chair and nestle with you while she continued her work. Dad would grab the tip of your finger and roll it between his thumb and index finger. It would appear absentminded but felt like a hug. Words about emotions don't really mean much to a child. We knew we were loved individually and as a group.

Big changes in our little lives were inevitable. Father left Providence College, and Dad accepted a large job in Cranston. Garden City was a planned community in the suburbs, one of the first in the nation. It progressed quickly, and he moved his business to the development's office building. We moved to a house there. It had four bedrooms and a two car garage on Morning Glory Drive. It was a new world spread before us and full of things to learn and people to meet.

Father was transferred to Ohio. We wrote and sent gifts to keep him close to us. He came to see us when he could during the summers. He was always dressed in his formal black suit and Roman collar and seemed like company, not the brother or uncle we had known. He blessed the new house. It was not the same except for the family rosary we knelt with him to say before he left. He led us in his familiar deep raspy voice that intoned the Hail Mary in a droney, chanted way like monks in a monastery. He emphasized the word "Hail" distinctively. If you closed your eyes and listened it seemed to be more than one man's voice and brought us back to years before. There was so much peace and security in those moments.

He made sure to speak with each of us separately, interested in how we were doing and what plans we were making for our futures. We would assure him that we continued to pray and to keep ourselves close to Jesus through Mary. He would hug us all tightly as he left and smile through his tears. We would promise to continue writing and remembering him in our prayers. We missed him deeply. There was no one like him in our new busy lives. We all cried also.

Surprisingly and wonderfully, Dad seemed to have brushed away all the tensions of their past relationship. Like any longtime pair of friends, they talked and laughed easily and eagerly. Mom cooked and fussed. They had a lot to share. We need not have been present, and one by one we left them to their visit.

Love is in the air as soldiers return.
Building boom predicted.
October 1, 1946

Chapter 14

In 1948 Mr. Nazarene Meloccaro purchased 500 acres of farmland and an abandoned graphite mine in western Cranston. He envisioned a modern community offering a safe, serene environment for a complete community providing all the necessities of suburban life on a public bus line fifteen miles from Providence. There was to be a development of 700 single family dwellings and 10 multifamily buildings. A future expansion of 500 houses would be added on a nearby parcel to be called Garden Hills.

He selected a garden theme for the development which would accommodate people of all ages and stations and which held family considerations first. Dad surveyed and plotted curving, flora named streets with no angular corners to keep traffic at safe speeds for children, and but four straight periphery streets for easy emergency vehicle access. Houses were angled where possible for privacy and room for planting areas provided on all of the lots. The architect, Adolf Kurze, designed homes in colonial, ranch,

Cape Cod, and split level styles of two to four and at times more bedrooms. After the homes were built maple trees were planted on each lot.

Two-story brick apartment buildings and duplex homes were included to accommodate all life styles and economic situations. All the homes had fireplaces, dishwashers, attached garages and breezeways. The latest in heating, electrical, and plumbing systems was installed. Land for the church, rectory, and public and parochial schools was donated to the city and diocese by the Meloccaro family.

The shopping center was laid out and begun simultaneously. The initial phase included a service station, pharmacy, supermarket, hardware store, women's dress shop, dry cleaner, barber shop, jeweler, appliance store, furniture store, children's clothing shop, delicatessen, haberdasher, the Outlet Co. Dept. Store, Woolworth's 5 and 10 Cent store, theater, bowling alley, creamery, and professional office building for doctors, dentists, lawyers, insurance agency, and optometrist. It was an intelligently considered and beautifully executed dream that the test of time has validated.

With completion of most of the heavy work on Garden City, Dad still worked with C. A. McGuire Engineering and became their Chief

Engineer. His responsibilities were great. He kept his private work going also. His successful work with McGuire was not rewarded and grew in scope.

Pressures built and the usually approachable Dad we loved became more and more tense and preoccupied. It was painful for Mom and all of us. She would shepherd us out of his way when necessary. His tension headaches intensified. There were times when he lost control and lashed out at Mom and us, then quickly and remorsefully settled down.

Soon he decided to leave McGuire and expand his own business to include large projects of the type he had been managing under McGuire, and before long he had all the work he could handle. A much larger staff and facility were acquired in Garden City, and our life and his were happier.

With all of our home training, we were sought out and allowed to babysit in our new neighborhood. Quite a liberal idea for the folks, it was a source of spending money and opportunity to test ourselves in a new arena. I did a lot of babysitting. Another welcome departure from our old restrictions was being allowed to take after school jobs in the shopping center a block from our home. We all enjoyed a variety of these employments. My best was as a soda jerk at Newport Creamery. This popular, bright, and friendly ice cream parlor was staffed by a manager, an adult bus boy, and four or five teens who waited on customers and created the delicious concoctions and sandwiches. We wore pastel colored uniforms and caps and were allowed seventy-five cents for mealtime shifts and twenty-five cents for a 15 minute break worth of anything we sold. I have a tiny aversion to banana splits for overdoing it in those days as the iconic glass boat dish had three scoops of ice cream and three toppings with whipped cream, pecans, and walnuts with three cherries on top for fifty cents. Their method of creating the perfect liverwurst sandwich is still a winner with my family.

The last shift of the day ended at 10 p.m. and was tasked with cleaning every inch of the place. The boys washed the floors and windows and scoured the grill. The girls cleaned all the stainless steel freezers, mixers, pumps, and inside and outside of the counters and cabinets. It took a while but didn't seem like work because the boys rolled the jukebox from the wall and rigged it to play continuously. We jitterbugged and sang through our tasks and made a memory to cherish today. Always in the back of my mind was what Daddy would think. This was too modern and not so genteel, especially the occasional ride home on the handlebars of Kenny's bike.

Garden City Shopping Center
Phase 1 – 1950

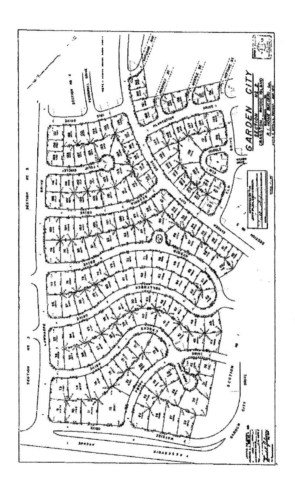

Garden City Section 2 of 5 plot plans submitted for Recording, June, 1948

It has been decided that the Sheraton-Biltmore Hotel's famed
Bacchante Room waitresses' costumes will no longer
display their lovely legs.
News Report, June, 1956

Chapter 15

It was inevitable. We were growing up.
Dad and Mom had to face lipstick, high heels,
dating. Tangee lip gloss was our first cosmetic
with it's lovely fruity scent. Supposed to enhance
your lips natural color, it was as subtle as possible.
Evelyn accompanied me to the drug store when I
asked to borrow her foundation makeup. In a very
sisterly and protective manner she firmly directed
the salesgirl to show me a product that would not
dry or irritate my complexion and that was light
and transparent. But Dad noticed and was
offended. "What have you got on your mouth?"
he'd say.

Mom was an active partner for us all, but
Dad hated these signs that we would eventually be
leaving and as much disliked the fact that we
would be departing in the arms of some man.
Older sisters were a help. Obvious to us all, this
was to be the reality of our teen years. Dad's
feelings about gentility, privacy, propriety, and the
qualities appropriate in a young lady were archaic

by 50's standards. He watched in quiet resignation and then grimly walked each of us down the aisle.

We all graduated from high school with honors. Nothing less was considered. It was inconceivable to any of us that our work or behavior would create even the slightest trouble or embarrassment for the family. Evelyn went off to college, studying for a medical assistant's career. Ori and Clare became nurses. Mariann and Jane went on to teach; and Peter got a degree in Civil Engineering, following his male forebears. Despite our own desires and the new horizons for women, none of us girls were told that we could be anything we wanted to be. Teaching, nursing, and secretarial careers were available.

Unlike my siblings, I had a very unsettled mind about my future. A great deal of pressure had been applied by the good Sisters at my high school who were sure I had a vocation and engendered a good deal of guilt about wanting anything else. Fathers Conaty and Sherer would comfort and discuss but only say they thought I had everything it took for a religious vocation, but I must be sure I wanted that life. I would know, they said. No help. I didn't know. It was as though no one, not even me, had a vision for my future except in the convent.

I thought of the military, but Dad's squinty stare when I mentioned it, disposed of that. Off to the nunnery for me!

There were three nurses in the family already and two teachers coming along. I loved children, but knew the limitations of a career in the classroom. I needed to clear my head and then try to visualize myself in other careers to realize my hopes for new experiences. The only way to find out and satisfy everyone was to once and for all settle the religious vocation issue. Really get a taste of it. I applied and with suitcase in hand went to the Dominican Sisters mother house and novitiate in Blauvelt, New York, to "try".

Dad and Mom drove me down. It was a very quiet ride. I had been instructed to say good-bye outside on arrival and to enter the novitiate alone. We said goodbye at the car. A young, bright, happy postulant welcomed and guided me through the beautiful mansion. She was warm and chatty and not much older than I. The appeal of that life blossomed in me again as I walked through the building with her. I had loved the Dominican Sisters who had taught grammar school. It became clear that this was the basis of my dilemma. Their beautiful poise and lovely white habits telling of the purity and peace that accompanied a lovely warmth and generosity in all their contact with us was the attraction. No Hollywood star carried herself with such radiance. I had developed a deep trusting relationship with them akin to what I had had with Fathers Sherer and Conaty and wanted to emulate and please them. Quickly a sense of remorse for not wholeheartedly and unselfishly embracing that life filled me.

This would be a tempting retreat to work things out, and I would be safe and not pressured in any way while there to commit to a vocation. A meeting with Mother Superior was scheduled. I was led to her study. It was a magnificent room with parquet floors, elegant carved warm colored wood walls and shelves in glass cabinetry, a cantilevered ceiling and graceful furnishings and oriental rugs. I was very nervous and could barely contain my turbulent emotions. I felt 'the principal's office' dread of everyone's childhood. She was young and elegant, warm, and intelligent. As with all sisters, she was gentle and serene. I was soon comfortable with her. We began our interview. It did not take long for her to lean forward and reach for my hand.

"You are not sure at all, are you?" she asked. This was the moment. No place or time for anything but cold, adult honesty. I explained that I knew I could live the community life happily and the rewards and contributions it would provide me but was held back from moving forward to it without a lot of regret that it would not be the full experience I thought life might offer and felt selfish and too worldly for not being willing to sacrifice those dreams.

"No, but I feel I am supposed to want a vocation and will be letting the Lord and others down if I fail to answer the call," I tearfully admitted. We chatted a few minutes longer, and she advised that I return home or could stay longer and continue to pray for guidance. They would contact my parents or arrange transportation if I wished. We stood, embraced, and she left with a sincere invitation to correspond with her or call at any time I wished to talk.

The postulant returned and was showing me to my room when I got a glimpse through the windows of our beige and white Plymouth with those big wings in the back waiting in the drive. Without being notified, they had returned for me. I never learned how they knew to return or why they came back for me. Had Dad heard me crying somehow as when in kindergarten? As soon as I dashed into the back seat choking back tears, he drove off. Mom was disappointed. It would have been wonderful to her to have a child with a vocation to religious life. I asked why they returned.

Dad said simply, "It wasn't right."

I couldn't have agreed more with him and felt like the sun was shining for the first time in over a year. In typical Cipolla fashion, no more was said. I needed to hear it was all right to close that door and should have had the courage to express that in my prayers and to everyone involved. It would have been uncomfortable for me and them to hear my feelings about rejecting the convent, and it wasn't the way we did things anyway.

Gentle Clare also felt the tug of a vocation and met with the Sisters of Charity but came to the same decision as I.

Late for college, I went on to business school which I thought offered the widest diversity of areas of future adventure. I could try anything. I wanted to test myself against yet unknown life styles, places, and experiences.

This was the 50's and the world was exploding with exciting new career paths. Electronics, communication, space, medicine, everything was developing at speeds that felt dangerous. It was not at the usual development progression of major inventive ideas that change a culture and lifestyles and to which thoughtful humans can easily adjust. The digital age was born and gave wonder and awe to young inquisitive minds. It seemed as though nothing was as it used to be. We learned new ways each day to do almost every aspect of life. You kept up or were left behind. The pace of life had trebled. We loved it. I wanted to find a place in it. It would take courage and curiosity. I felt I had both and with business training I could find the life I wanted and could make a useful contribution.

We had not been allowed to preen much and humility was highly valued at home; but to judge from the parade of young men who called, it didn't matter. We had been raised in a chaste, respectful, unpampering home and expected to pitch in quietly. We all knew how to cook well. What more could a man want. We would all become capable mothers and wives who kept good homes, loved and respected our in-laws, and were loving full partners to our husbands. We would all continue our work careers.

One by one Dad reluctantly walked us down the aisle of St. Mark's Church. He fussed about the pageantry and particularly his role in it. He offered each of us a handsome bribe to elope quietly. None of us accepted. Mom insured with enthusiasm that each of us had a beautiful day with all the trimmings to start our married life.

Dad and Mom had doubled their family's size in little over ten years with the marriages of their children. Everyone fit into the family comfortably, and wonderful relationships developed in a Cipolla network that continues to expand. In time grandchildren aplenty were added to our many happy and lively family gatherings. Each one adds a new and special ingredient to the mix.

I met and married Raymond, an Electrical Engineer at IBM. Ray was rock solid and an ardent suitor. Roses were delivered prior to his arrival back in Rhode Island from New York each Friday. He came with chocolates which I knew would be shared before I returned home from our date. I got tired of the liberties taken with my things. His daily letters were also enjoyed. I was warned to be less sensitive and secretive. I understood the attraction of a romance to my siblings and wanted to share. We all sensed the beginning of the separation to come for me. But, it was very serious to me. He wanted a life partner in the expanding opportunities ahead of him. I wanted someone who would show me new worlds and who would try new things beside me. We would venture together and discover a new life.

After our October wedding we rented an artist's guest house/studio in Woodstock, New York's, mountains and bought two German Shepard dogs named Hans and Heidi. Our first home was a small, new cottage composed of one large room with a kitchen alcove and Japanese screens to create a bedroom. The bathroom had a bidet and the living room a model's platform and spotlights which we were allowed to remove. It was beautifully hidden in the forest and had a perfect view of Overlook Mountain. On many clear nights in winter we watched the leaping kaleidoscope of the aurora borealis in silence.

The world now involved in a space race.
Soviets launch the Sputnik satellite.
October 4, 1957

Chapter 16

A tidal wave of technical specialists landed in the small towns of upstate New York. Housing, services, and women were in short supply. IBM, GE, and other giants in electronics vied for talent. We went to IBM and both worked on an Air Force/NORAD air defense support effort. IBM's SAGE computer, the brains of this effort, covered acres of building space. Pluggable units, today's electronic chip, contained vacuum tubes and parts similar to a radio, and worked together throughout the system. A good deal of heat was generated by this massive machine, and mountains of punched computer cards were read in the process.

My first view of the facility was when Ray drove me to my job interview. Startling was the huge black BOMARC missile perched in launch position on the main building lawn. Security was high, and FBI clearances began before I was hired with interviews of our neighbors and a close look at my life to that date. I'm sure those agents were bored. This was the adventure I hoped existed beyond the world I knew and the options I had had after school. There was a buzz in that

Catskill air. Engineers from all parts of the world had left family and familiar territory to use their educations. Social and work associations were rich and interesting. On everyone's mind seemed to be the next big thing for the digital age. Most co-workers had an idea or invention confidentially shared with a few trusted colleagues. The future was at their fingertips, and digital potential was unlimited. Everyone wanted a piece.

Ray and his close friends were involved in discussions focusing on the transistor, printed circuit, microchip, and unthought of uses for digital software technology. The big hurdle was start-up capital. There was a pot of gold waiting for any and all who could come up with a new invention and funding. I wanted a home and family, and viewed the enthusiasm warily but was willing to wait and encouraged Ray.

We were loving, respectful partners and enjoyed each other's company at all times. We had made a prenup that as a team we would protect and honor one another. A little sensitive but we stuck to it. We had witnessed too often the sadness and humiliation in social settings as one spouse shared their mate's personal foibles or mistakes. However, we did disagree on the subject of "FUN". The word itself irritated Ray and was in heavy use. We were invited for cocktails and some "FUN" at friends' homes. I thought we could have a little "FUN" on weekends. We all worked very hard. There was something job related to do at home each night and often study for advanced degrees was waiting.

As we approached a free weekend one Friday night returning home from work, I suggested we have some "fun" this weekend. He looked at me seriously and asked "Just what does that mean?" He said he hears it all the time. He wanted to know what wasn't fun about our weekends. "What is the fun everyone wants to have?" he said. Our folks didn't have "fun", but we had more money and less worries than they. We weren't so dog tired at the end of the day and were younger. Was this Dad's "Nonsense"?

His photos of playing in bands and flying with buddies seemed as though he should indeed know what "fun" was. Instead he enjoyed listening to jazz records, playing his trumpet, flying a plane, or driving to some jazz group's event. I meant having parties, going to clubs, mixing with friends. I admit to being more socially inclined than he. Today, dear Ray would be called a nerd or geek and not the cool cat he was then. Without too much difficulty we did get that settled, and as the years went by each week was peppered with people and events that were "fun" and without drugs or drunkenness. He definitely knew what having "fun" was. It was loosening up that we enjoyed and dropping the reserve necessary at work.

I had wanted to entertain and engage in some of the light-hearted games that were popular. We did that when we partied with family. It was a natural continuation for Ray of childhood relationships. He was reluctant to loosen up that much with acquaintances. We worked it out slowly. I loved to cook, and we used that to cultivate close friendships with Ray totally involved. After a year or so we were giving big parties with wonderful conversation and whatever games our guests wanted to play. "FUN" was a pressure valve, and he needed its release more than I. He was onboard. Even after the children came, we continued this time for ourselves, and the children watched and helped as we lived our adult lives just as I had watched and helped my parents.

And so it went happily for three years. Much of the newest technology was being developed in Massachusetts along Rte. 128. Military contracts with major electronic firms involved defense systems and the space program. We both were hired by MIT, and built our first home in Carlisle, a small town adjacent to Concord, Massachusetts, near Boston. We built the house ourselves after work and on weekends. Family helped when they could. After a contractor erected the shell, we plastered, laid oak floors, installed the electrical wiring, tiled the bathrooms, painted, and anything else that was necessary. It was possible to be in Rhode Island more easily and keep better contact with our families. Their visits to us were frequent. Our son, John, and daughter, Rachel, were born there.

When military contracts were awarded to companies and facilities in California in the late sixties, the Rte. 128 electronics boom ended. We sold our home and moved to a town on the Rhode Island border. Back home! The children were able to experience the sweetness of a large extended family. I had the companionship and help that I had always enjoyed. Ray pursued an Ocean Engineering degree and finance studies. His real love was technical analysis of the stock market. He switched to that field of endeavor.

Father came to visit us when he was in town. The children met him, and warmed to him as quickly as we had at their ages. There were still the familiar Oh Henry bars and fishing stories. His warmth and generosity hadn't ebbed. His sincere interest in our welfare, both physical and spiritual, hadn't lessened. His hallmark teary bear hug was as tight and loving as ever.

I learned to imitate a barber fairly well for Ray when we first moved Woodstock. The invasion of engineers and scientists to the small mountain towns in that area badly overtaxed what services there were. Ray just wanted a neat clean haircut as was the expectation at IBM. We ordered a clipper set from Sears Roebuck. With his encouragement and obvious lack of concern about the outcome, I learned to taper and neaten his lovely hair. I added another skill to my repertoire of handy tricks. When he learned of this, Dad, who never enjoyed the ministrations of a barber, didn't visit one again. Mom thrilled me with the gift of her cherished father's striped barber's cloth. Dad would come to me, or I would take my barber's bag to him regularly.

He offered this service to Father, and each time he would visit, I would cut his hair also. As with Dad and Ray, these were chatty visits. Usually quiet men they relaxed under the striped cloth, and I relished the discussions. Dad always hid some money somewhere in the house so well afterward that I might not find it for several days. I could imagine his mischievous smile as he hid it. When I complained, he said it was worth a million not to have to go to a barber. It was worth a million to me too.

The sales tax is regressive in taking mostly from the least
able to pay, and a state lottery does the same.
April, 1961, Radio News

Chapter 17

When the folks received an invitation to a testimonial event for Father's 50th anniversary in the priesthood, Mom and Dad were unable to attend, so my sister Ori and I agreed to represent the family. We flew to Detroit and stayed at a hotel across the street from the impressive GM headquarters.

The event was to begin with a concelebrated high Mass in the parish church where he had worked since arriving in Detroit. It was in one of the poorest sections of Detroit. Approaching it filled us with dread as we passed razed block after block and people huddled around barrels of burning trash. It was an area similar to many industrial centers across the country which were undergoing a major revival. But what was he doing here? An esteemed friend who left Providence College as an accomplished, erudite man dedicated to academic work, a professor of chemistry and physics, and also a scholar of homiletics seemed not to belong in what we were seeing. It didn't take long to know he was practicing what he preached.

We arrived in time for this obviously special Mass to judge by the carefully prepared printed programs we received, the altar flower and candle arrays, and the full choir. It was my first indication of how deeply he had touched the hearts of the many joyous faces in the church. There was no doubt that the special love and attention given in all generosity and humility to us was not because we were that special to him but maybe because we were willing to receive it. And, he looked to me to be the living embodiment of all those little religious talks the point of which was to do good works in His name and to keep God with us always. He will be as comforting and generous with His love and help as Father was to any in need.

Here, he was assistant pastor and parish priest, which is the most wearying and difficult position in the priesthood for someone of his age.

Mass proceeded as is usual in any Catholic church in the world. His familiar raspy voice was clear and strong and a joy to hear. The pastor of this parish, a cheerful looking man of middle age, assisted Father as concelebrant. As Communion of the faithful approached, he stepped to the mike and announced that Communion could be received in the hand and that all those who wished that should approach him. Father Sherer would distribute to those who would receive on the tongue. We approached Father Sherer.

A parishioner explained to us later that Father was troubled by some of the edicts of Vatican Council II, especially distributing the host into a person's hand. A priest's hands had been consecrated, and his alone should be entrusted to protect the host. A temporary compromise must have been reached with his Dominican superior and the local Bishop whereby he said Mass and offered Communion in the traditional manner if another priest was there to distribute in the hand.

Many issues leapt to mind that we will never know answers to. How strongly did he object and to whom? What other restrictions might he have had imposed on his hieratic ministry? I remembered the reverence and deep concentration he showed when saying Mass or praying at our home. His solemnity and devotion were contagious, even for Dad. I felt respect and pride. He had such deep solid beliefs and dedication to those priestly principles that he felt strongly could not be violated. They were the bedrock of his faith and vocation, his character and life. He had often warned in concert with Daddy that times change, but most changes are short lived and often hard to reverse. We were to be steadfast to basic truths and common sense. Whatever would finally be decided, I knew he would happily obey.

After a laudatory introduction by his Pastor, Father delivered a heartwarming sermon, peppered with humor and appreciation. He was led down the aisle and everyone followed him to the school auditorium. It was carefully and beautifully decorated with balloons, bunting, banners, and flowers. Especially impressive were huge arches made of large black and white balloons that were about ten balloons deep and stood firm as arches in a cathedral's apse. The head table was there.

I watched feeling like a stranger as testimonials from local officials, church dignitaries, and parishioners followed one after the other and each speaker told of the personal deep connections that he had forged. The love and respect in that hall was palpable. These were people of all ages and stations in the community. Very touching was the number of possibly homeless and people of simple means who wanted to express their love and thanks. Their testimonials spoke of cold winters and late hours when Father would minister to them at places he should have feared to go and with whatever they needed that he could procure, from where they never could tell. He worked on foot and alone. This was a very poor parish, but had dedicated and selfless people of means and ability who poured their resources into keeping St. Dominic's Parish vibrant. Father had found his calling and had many needy parishioners to whom he could apply his boundless generosity. They called him Detroit's "Apostle of the Poor".

He spent as much time as he could with us but was in great demand. He asked for news of Dad and Mom and every last one of us. We then said good bye and as usual, he hugged us very tightly and cried. It had been a wonderful experience.

We continued our correspondence and Christmas and St. Joseph's day gifts. He seemed to be healthy and unchanged. His workload had increased with changes in staffing at the parish many times; but his dedication to the needy never waned.

Chapter 18

In the '70s Dad sold his business and retired. He was not a man who could be idle or enjoy participating in a sport except baseball games on the radio. He had few friends with whom he wished to spend time. He felt confined to the house. The winters were very difficult for both him and Mom. His sensitivity to drafts which caused sinus headaches and arthritis pain in his joints made most excursions painful. He had severe arterial sclerosis which was worsened by the cold.

Not people who took trips often, surprisingly they tried the Florida Keys for a few weeks one winter, and it was just what Dad had been looking for. The pace was slower and quieter. He could sit on a secluded beach and soak up the warm sun. He spent peaceful hours enjoying the nearly untouched tropical environment. He marveled while demonstrating how he regained flexibility in his hands and fingers there when they had been arthritis stiff in the cold of Rhode Island.

Eventually they purchased a home with a swimming pool and dock on the Atlantic side of a small key south of Islamorada. They would keep their Garden City home for trips up north.

When the time came to move down, I volunteered to help with the driving and settling in. At the first key with just 75 miles to go, Mom spotted a farmer's stand at the side of the road and wanted to bring fresh fruit and vegetables to begin stocking her new empty kitchen. It was on a narrow strip of highway verge tucked into the mangrove growth at the southern part of the Everglades. When we left the car, we were welcomed by a small honey and white colored solidly built little puppy, probably a Chihuahua mix about a year old.

The vendor said it had been abandoned and would probably not survive the night, be eaten by the gators, that is. Shaking his head he lamented that he tried to take care of these discarded pets, but over the years there had been too many. This little mix didn't have a chance. Of course, it nuzzled and whimpered and looked bright and adorable. Mom and Dad were stunned by that reality of their new environment and the puppy's fate. We knew we couldn't leave him. Sympathetic glances were exchanged. Always softhearted, Dad would stop if a large bug or hapless bird hit our windshield. He once left us in the car on a dodgy street as he ran to help a man lying on the sidewalk in the throes of a seizure. Found in Homestead, adopted when Mom said, "let's go home" to him, and honoring the ancient poet, the puppy became Homer, loved friend and comfort to them.

Homer was a bridge between their daily lives in Rhode Island where several and sometimes all family members stopped by or called and to a life where that was impossible. It was probably a relief to have uninterrupted time together and a less lively pace. The puppy stood proxy for all of us by demanding care and love. His needs would be met willingly and would set a satisfying routine. He would entertain them with his antics and comfort them with his affection and dedication. He'd be someone Mom could talk to when Dad wanted his cherished quiet. He would cuddle with her on the couch for her midday nap. Dogs in the north despise pesky squirrels who overrun their yards. Homer had a different quarry. He developed an instant hate for the many sand crabs on the beach and entertained Dad with his futile attempts to catch or dig them up.

Our parents each built new, rewarding lives. Dad dedicated his efforts to bringing the property up to pristine, modern levels. Mom volunteered at the hospital and enjoyed decorating and keeping the elegant house.

We visited them often. She missed her home in Rhode Island and being near her children and grandchildren. To remedy this, an arrangement was devised whereby Mom would return in the summers for a while and a grandson would replace her so she wouldn't worry about Dad's being alone. "To keep peace," he agreed. Solitude was paradise for him, but this minor compromise was necessary.

It worked well and continued with most of the grandsons taking a turn. They returned rosy brown and somehow changed. A sense of responsibility for themselves and the confidence that required was evident. They all grew up a good deal in Dad's no nonsense world. It was a wonderful one-on-one experience for them which their granddad filled with work, fun, and life lessons. He did not waste time on pleasantries or sentimentalities. They got their hair tussled or finger squeezed, and they knew what that meant just as we had.

He involved them in projects he had postponed until he had the extra willing male help of these boys. He let them feel his appreciation and approval in the same quiet ways he showed us as children. There is no better feeling of acceptance than that. It was a gentle boot camp and family rite of passage for those lucky boys, and they knew they were helping their grandparents live a new life. After work they explored new restaurants together as a companionable treat.

Chapter 19

Occasionally Father would visit Mom and Dad from Detroit when he could get away and had use of a car. He had a sister in Sarasota, and she would lend him a small car to drive to the Keys. He loaded it up with gifts and would arrive beaming and happy at their door. They were happy to see him, even Dad. Their lengthy, amiable talks resumed.

One of our visits to their Keys home coincided with a visit from Father. He must have telephoned or written to them to advise of his vacation, and maybe they told him that we would be there also with our new boat. We were learning to sail. Living on beautiful Narragansett Bay, the lure of sailing is strong. The children were of an age to participate, and we thought it a good family sport. We approached this new endeavor seriously, as we did everything. The Coast Guard course and certification was the natural beginning, and all four of us enrolled and passed. Ray continued with navigation, and I became c.p.r. certified.

Ragbagging (i.e. sailing as opposed to motoring "stinkpots") was our choice. We had enjoyed sailing with friends on the bay. We purchased a Dyer Dhow training sloop. It was 12 feet long and had everything necessary to learn to sail a larger boat. We bought a trailer for it and would day trip on the bay enjoying the excitement of riding the wind. The small boat did little to dull the feel and movement of the wind and water. We all loved it and the rich family time together.

The trip to the Keys was a twofold venture. We would see the folks and skim the waters off Florida. Our usual travel to Florida was a non-stop drive. This trip we hitched the trailer with boat to the car and left home at 4 a.m. to get through heavy traffic areas in the north before the morning rush. Our usual path was mostly on Rtes. 1 and 301 through the southern states. We passed through towns called Fayetteville, Lumberton, Jessup, etc. When I hear them now, I am filled with wonderful memories. We would be away two weeks and promised the children a stay at Disney World on the return trip. Tickets and reservations were arranged.

Driving through the deep south during the night was enchanted with unusual radio programs, local news, talk, and music. It was a time to talk at length of current issues, plans, and personal feelings unspoken in the rush of our routine lives. Ray had rigged an extension to the back seat allowing the children to sleep comfortably with pillows and blankets. It was cozy and fun.

Since before our wedding we had developed a "what if…" pass time for long rides to savor changes and dream for the future or deal with a current issue. Its cousin "the little things" was to imagine random details possible in the plan or goal whether bizarre, feasible, lovely, or horrible. Ray would introduce these chats with something like, "What if we move to…" or "What if I return to graduate school". Unfortunately, we never what-if'ed "should one of us die".

We spelled each other at the wheel for napping when possible, and the children read and enjoyed the sights. I packed roast beef and ham sandwiches, PBJ's, water, ice, fresh baked egg biscuits, pizza slices, snacks, candy, cokes, and sweet bread with butter, fruit, juices--all in individual size servings.

Frequent stops were made, and it took us a full day and most of the next to reach the Keys. Rte. 95 was paved in just small sections of highway near large cities, and detours and construction added slow-downs to the trip. Most of the ride was on Routes 301 and 1 which covered the rural south until Jacksonville, then on Route 1A through Indian River orange groves and all the eastern coastline Florida resort cities.

City names like Rocky Mount and Jacksonville still hold romance for me. We had breakfasts of grits, biscuits and gravy, with delicious ham and eggs; stopped at South of the Border; read the Burma Shave signs; bought coffee and ice cream at Stuckey's; and pecans at roadside stands in front of neat small tin houses on crates.

It was late March. In Virginia, the Carolinas, and Georgia, trees and flowers were in bloom. Magnolia, lilac, wisteria, laurel, and fruit trees painted a lovely colorful landscape so different from the still frozen dead-looking north. The scent in these places was almost overpowering, and in the Florida orange groves intoxicating.

However, the first night in North Carolina at 2 a.m. our sturdy Plymouth Fury's water pump blew spraying the windshield. Ray put the wipers on, and we eased to the side of the road. There were no street lights along rural two lane Rte. 301, and the semi's whizzed by shaking the heavy car. The children slept. We looked at one another, and an icy chill ran through me. Using a good deal of our water for the radiator, we took off again hoping for a nearby gas station or small town. The map indicated that our next city was Rocky Mount, and we headed that way. After a very short time, we needed to add more water.

This took us a little closer. When we had used up all our supply, we were on the outskirts of that city, a major junction for many north/south and east/west routes. However, we were no nearer a service station.

While I bit my knuckles in the dark car, valiant Ray took the gallon water jug and approached a house, located an outside faucet, and filled the jug. We made it closer until that also was exhausted. He repeated the maneuver at a small white church this time. No dogs barked and no gun shots or shouts were heard. We stole water from one more building before we rolled into Rocky Mount at 4 a.m. Giddy with relief, we remarked on what could have happened. We were Italian and Catholic and laughed with relief at the silliness of those old stories.

The all night diner/truck stop looked cheerful and busy. Ray went in for coffee though we both could have used a brandy. He came back in good humor and said the proprietor had promised to wake the owner of the auto parts store. The mechanic was not scheduled to work this day, but he would see what he could do. What wonderful people! Similar assistance for someone from out of state at a diner or auto parts store at home was not probable. Our only worry was how much this generous help would cost.

Within the hour, a very pleasant owner of the auto parts store arrived and went with Ray to unlock his store and to get the right part. The bill was under $40. Similarly, the mechanic did come, and his services didn't cost as much. They waved us off by 6:30 after coffee and conversation and breakfast for John and Rachel. The experience was like being in a Gunsmoke episode where the whole town rallies to help a stranger in trouble, preceded by a bit of nightmarish Twilight Zone. We shared this memory many times with friends. It still feels remarkable. I am deeply indebted to those softhearted southerners who were so generous to strangers in need. God bless Dixie.

We arrived in the early evening at the folks' house and settled in comfortably. There was a very warm welcome. We sat and talked as long as we could stay awake. The place looked beautiful. Daddy had repaired, replaced, and beautified everything. His puttering now was merely care of all the tropical plants and trees they had added. He had papaya, lemon, Key line, orange, avocado, the ubiquitous coconut, mango, and a sea of flowering vines and shrubs. All producing generously for him.

Next morning after breakfast and a guided tour of all the changes that had been made, Dad helped us launch the dhow. The short steep concrete ramp in the lawn stopped at the beach sand. Keeping the car from spinning in the sand was important. We got the boat into the water and tied her to the dock. It was picturesque with its mast up and white hull bobbing on the turquoise water as though it had always belonged there.

It was a beautiful, clear Keys morning with the ever present stiff breeze scented with tropical musk and ocean salt warmed by a bright sun. The sky is an entity you're always conscious of in the Keys. The constant movement of clouds against a vivid blue ground masks and unmasks the strong sunlight producing a quickly changing reality. You squint and refocus constantly. Very soon that tropical torpor develops and leads you to a chaise to loll in the warmth. The night sky presents an awesome array of stars to dazzle the mind and flood the senses. Their brilliance, density, and seeming nearness allows you to see a wonderfully tangled celestial depth. It's a spectacle difficult to turn from and awesome to the eye and soul.

We went for a short sail, Dad and Mom demurring. Drinks and snacks were waiting when we returned. The lazy pace of an afternoon of swimming and napping preceded dinner and then TV and bed. It began to feel like the vacation we needed so badly. Ray especially had to rid himself of the heavy stress he carried in his work as the bank's investment analyst. Like Dad, he was driven by his work and not one to seek a way to relieve its impact. He just pushed through single-mindedly. He was tightly wound.

On the third day of our stay, Father Sherer arrived. Mom had taken a call from him. He was leaving Sarasota and would drive right through until he reached us. His transportation was a small blue hatchback that sported a good deal of body damage and evidence of a dip in a canal. With a huge smile and kisses and hugs for all of us, he looked quickly around the front yard, linked arms with Dad and commented appreciatively on all the improvements that had been made. Dad was happy to see him and to share convivially.

He was obviously delighted to be with us and on leave from his duties. This was the family friend, adopted uncle to us kids, and not just the family's special priest. He wore a short sleeved plaid shirt and chinos. His loafers were worn on the outside edges as proof positive that despite signs of aging this was Father. He looked considerably older and gaunt with all white hair giving him a Bavarian fairytale character look. Hard work and purpose were evident in his stooped head and fast stride, but the rosy cheeks and sparkling blue eyes told of his good health and vigorous spirit. Regarding his general condition, I had heard only of some arthritis. He was thinner.

He was as ebullient and happy as ever.

We lugged his suitcase and black suit in a garment bag out of the back seat while he fumbled with the trunk lid which seemed to be stuck somehow. Ray helped pry it open. He and Dad pulled their chins down and raised their eyebrows in surprise when they saw the provisions that filled that space. There was a sack of grapefruit, a case of bourbon, a box of Oh Henry's, bottles of wine, and a case of beer. A lot of booze for social drinkers. Bringing citrus fruit to anyone in Florida seemed odd until he said he had learned of a new refreshing drink to make with them. The generosity of his sister was evident.

Mom and I worked in the kitchen to get dinner on the table while Father was settling his belongings. He was to stow his gear in the front guest closet but insisted on sleeping on the living room sofa refusing vehemently to take the small dressing room off the upstairs bedroom which Ray and I were using or to displace any one of us. The living room couch was a pull-out where Mom had planned to relocate the children. He wouldn't hear of moving the children there either, insisting on it for himself.

When all the arrangements were concluded, Father used Mom's electric juicer to make the adults his new drink. It was half fresh squeezed grapefruit juice and half bourbon on ice garnished with mint, etc. I loved it and make it still. Dad, Mom, and Ray didn't take a second.

Conversation around the dinner table was lively. His gravelly laugh was loud and so easy. We all felt tension we didn't know we held slipping away. Each of us had questions for him, and he wanted an update from everyone. With a remarkable recollection of what each of us had told him at our last communication, he asked for progress. It was an honor and blessing, a sign of his care and love. Dinner was not merely relaxed and leisurely, it ate up most of the evening. Though tired, Mom asked if he wouldn't please lead us in prayer as years before. We all knelt and responded to his chanted lead. This had always been a fitting and heartwarming bedtime prayer, and we left them and went to our rooms. Ray and the children were surprised and respectful.

Chapter 20

As Floridians respond to "How's things down there?", "Another day in Paradise!" began with a soft call from Mom to come down and join them at Mass. She had arranged an altar area on the dining room table, and Father had opened his leather bag and put his chalice, cruets, and platen on linens next to his missal. The Last Supper on our dining room table! Dad and John were recruited as altar boys and did a good job. Dad had been going with Mom to church on Sundays, and strange for us to hear, had been asked to pass the basket which he did without complaint. Retirement had softened him even about religion and was lovely for me to witness. His ease and friendliness with Father was genuine and minus any sign of hesitance. I don't doubt though that there might have been a tiny amount of wariness in him.

After Mass, we served breakfast outside by the pool. Then Dad and Father sat under Grandpa's striped barber's cloth for a chatty shearing. Instead of the laid back pace of last night's dinner, Father wanted to be busy. He asked Dad about projects that were underway, and Ray about the boat and fishing. Dad said there was nothing needing doing (I understood, "needing your help"), and that Father should relax and enjoy the amenities at our vacationing disposal. Working around the house at his own pace was how Dad had built his new life. It was a pleasure for him. He didn't want to relinquish control of it or rush through something that was a joy every step of the way to him.

Father didn't push the issue and asked Ray to show him the boat. I recognized the old pattern of his contributing in some little way to repay Dad and Mom's generosity, and in a way allow him a stake in the family. I also recognized remnants of the reluctance of old in the folks, Mom anticipating a conflict, and Dad knowing he would lose any attempt to squelch Father's charitable instincts. He couldn't take himself off to his office so he would have to do what he could to minimize the intrusion.

The boat was declared a very seaworthy little vessel, and Father blessed it at my request. Everyone lined up on the dock, and he waded to the boat with his holy water bottle. Mom whispered something about the moray eels and manta rays, but I don't think he heard her.

Father and Ray planned for some sport fishing either that day or within the next couple of days. Father would seek out bait and sportsmen to get as much local knowledge as he could beforehand. Ray wanted to spend some time on the phone and update his stock movement charts. That meant a run somewhere for the WSJ and a Barron's, and an hour or so for me to help update the charts.

The children had no need for diversion. The pool and beach kept their attention, and Mom fussed over them with refreshments, hats, and sun tan lotions. She had a plan for the two of us to go to a local VFW charity bingo that night so she was planning an early dinner. It was always with silent reluctance that I left with her for a bingo, but with happiness that I returned. She appreciated the company very much and loved to introduce her children to acquaintances. It was a big payoff for so little effort, and I did treasure those times alone with her.

Father's fishing trip in the dhow was planned for Tuesday mid-morning. Mom and I had shopped the day before for picnic items and prepared filled aa cooler with drinks, sandwiches, and snacks. On Tuesday there was excitement in everyone's voice. The day was perfect with the expected clear steady trade winds. No storms were predicted, and the sea was calm.   Ray, Dad, Father, and the children went to the bait shop.

Around 10:30 we loaded the boat, and Father, John, and Rachel climbed aboard.   I helped Ray remove the land lines, and he attached the sheets, lowered the center board, and set the helm.   He jumped aboard, raised the sail, and grabbed the tiller.   The canvas caught the wind immediately and filled out for trimming. Skillfully, he moved the little boat away from the dock in one smooth drift and the sails tightened on a comfortable beat straight out into the Atlantic.   Waving back to the sailors from the dock, Dad and I smiled approvingly.   Mom signed one of her farewell crosses over them and mumbled a prayer.   Everyone on board settled in their places with life jackets clipped tightly and turned toward the horizon.

We watched for several minutes as the little boat made surprising speed and diminished in size against that huge turquoise expanse of Caribbean Sea.   Soon we could see only a small triangle of white and then nothing.   Mom had returned to the house.   Dad wasn't smiling, and I could feel the cold creep of anxiety.   An hour passed.   Mom brought us coffee and after searching the horizon trying to spot them asked in alarm where they were.

"God damn it. They're way out of range. Must be miles out." Dad fumed. "The gulf stream is not far off. It curves here and meanders. For Christ's sake. Fishing! What God damn nonsense."

"Good heavens!" she mumbled. "Take it easy."

I didn't need to be reminded. Ray and I had thought yesterday that we could see the change in color and the rise of the gulf stream through our binoculars. He would not go anywhere near it, I was sure. But he didn't know these shark infested waters. We hadn't seen many sail boats from the shore, although large powerful sport boats were zipping everywhere. If there was a problem someone would see them and help. We had agreed on a two or three-hour fishing excursion. I especially felt that the children shouldn't be exposed to the sun that long. I had thought then that they would be within sight the whole time.

Dad got his binoculars and the vigil began. Mom alternated between silent praying and tempered worry. There were no cell phones then, and the dhow didn't have an emergency radio on board.

"Father is there," she said hopefully. That was as good as God at the helm, right? Dad's experiences over the years with God's helping

Father in everyday situations started his check twitching, and he began pacing off his frustration and concern.

I trusted my husband to be able to captain our children back safely. After four more hours of no sightings, all of us were distraught. Dad made an inquiry to the Coast Guard who said they would keep a lookout for them. It was a horribly long afternoon.

Finally around 4:30 we could focus the binoculars on a tiny white spot straight ahead that very gradually increased in size. It was the dhow. With what amounted to a celebration, we hugged each other and wiped tears of relief. None of us could take our eyes off that white spot and watched on tiptoes until we could make out the four heads bouncing toward us.

They pulled alongside the dock. Father loudly greeted us and was obviously delighted with the trip. John and Rachel each lifted buckets of fish.

"Wonderful trip! Yellow tail! Lots of them." Father said.

Ray didn't move from his seat at the tiller. He passed the lines to me and then some gear. Father and the children unloaded their catch and climbed over to wade ashore. Ray didn't move. He looked up at me and sort of smiled. I knew that apologetic, pained expression. My heart sank. He couldn't move. The bouncing had triggered his vacation curse. Lower back muscle spasm in it's most painful manifestation had locked onto him again. It was a result of the tension and stress of his work, physicians explained. An Achilles heel with no remedy. It would be alternating heat and cold packs and flat on his back for days. Unable to lift his body or walk easily, he needed to rely on us which plunged him into an irritable funk to add to his pain.

Dad and I helped him lift his legs one at a time over the side of the boat and using his arms and the dock he slipped into the water. We slowly got him to the pool area where he tried to straighten himself by stretching against a chair back. This condition is evidenced by the huge swelling that develops on one side of his back pulling him into a letter C shape. He would suffer constant pain as with a charley horse in his calf.

Father was solicitous. Mom fussed but was obviously joyous over their safe return.

"Tsk tsk!' Shaking his head Dad grumbled, "We could have bought that fish for a few dollars. What God damned nonsense! Take those chances! Risk lives!"

Dad was still shaking his head as he wandered away from everyone. I got Ray into a hot shower and bed and looked for a drink for both of us.

Downstairs Mom and Father were cleaning the fish. It had been a very successful fishing trip. Father was still thrilled at the quantity of the catch and the thrill of the location, his lifelong dream of fishing the Keys' reef. The children had many excited stories of their prowess to relate. Some of the fish was cooked for dinner, some went into the freezer as another gift from Father, and some readied to take to his sister in Sarasota. Dad joined us for dinner but didn't eat much. Ray didn't want anything but took another drink. He knew he would be trapped in that room for days. Mom brought him a nightstand bell to summon help. He wouldn't use it.

Chapter 21

Florida's Chamber of Commerce must be speaking of the Keys when they boast of continuous wonderful weather. Wednesday and Thursday were exploring and pool play days. Ray worked on his charts and made phone calls from bed. Dad resumed his usual Florida routine of upkeep on the property which might more aptly be called manicuring.

Father said Mass again the next morning in the dining room with everyone present except Ray. Father brought Communion to him in bed. Mom wanted to go shopping, but I couldn't leave with her. Father volunteered to rinse off the boat and help stow the sail, etc. There would be no more sailing this trip.

Dad had decided to handle a little problem in the pool pump's plumbing. I am not exactly sure what it was, perhaps new filters as the children were using the pool. He needed some items from the hardware store in Tavernier. Also, Father had noticed a drip in the upstairs bathtub. When he saw Dad preparing to leave he said he would like to join him but didn't say anything about the drip.

When they returned, Dad was obviously annoyed. The brief stop at the store had been successful, but it wasn't until the proprietor insisted on giving Dad a discount on the articles he had selected that Dad remembered saying "Father". A tug of war ensued over the bill. Wanting peace, Dad relented. He fumed later that these small businesses depended on their local customers and couldn't afford a discount for anyone. He was incensed and returned alone the next day to return the discount. I would like to have known what he said to the proprietor, but do know it was probably not a condemnation of Father's actions.

Father didn't hear the exchange that followed between Dad and Mom. As in many instances in years past Mom pleaded that Father was only trying to help. He did not have the money to show his appreciation for our hospitality and for his needed vacation except in these little helpful ways. Dad said he did not want to hear that word "help" anymore.

After lunch, Dad got to work on his plumbing issue in the garage area utility room. Unbeknownst to him, Father went up to the top floor bathroom and began fixing the leak.

Somehow a rupture occurred in the water supply pipe to the upper level, and a flood began that inundated the area below where Dad was working and further overtaxed an aging septic system. The turn-off valves were corroded by the salty environment and did not work. The yard turned into an unsavory swamp area and the utility room and garage were flooded.

Dad's emergency call to a plumbing company prompted the quick arrival of a truck and various equipment to pump, dig up, and temporarily fix the problem. The pool water had been compromised so it too had to be pumped. Iffy house plumbing and no swimming pool would be the situation for a few days. But we could get by. Father was very apologetic and was reassured that it was all right, could have happened at any time. Dad's attitude indicated he just wanted quiet and to be left alone.

Ray was still confined to bed and not able to help. He and Dad over the years of our marriage had developed a mutual respect and ability to work together on these kinds of problems when Dad asked for his help in all the electrical, carpentry, and house handy skills Ray had developed. He could have been a buffer and help for Dad. He knew it and regretted anew his helplessness.

Friday's first glow of sunrise was brighter than up north and woke me quickly. It was the end of our stay. I quietly left the house not wanting to disturb anyone else. But, to my joy I found Dad wandering about the yard with a coffee mug in one hand and a cigarette in the other. What a thrill to be alone with him at dawn again.

He was surveying the chaos in his once pristine retirement paradise. It was truly shocking and indecent to see its innards revealed for everyone to see and as sad as a defiled piece of art. Piles of dirt and coral covered the grass. The pool was empty and its plumbing exposed. A pipe to the house had been dug up which had required smashing through the pool apron and walkways and knocking out a big hole in the house footing. He didn't seem as upset as I would have thought. Here was a man who had obviously had a lifetime of train wrecks to handle. He seemed to be saying time is short, enjoy even the messes.

"What are you going to do about all this?" I asked.

"Get it fixed. I've known it needed replacing. These islands are coral and don't handle or hold as much as up home. It'll work out", he said.

"I think Father is very sorry." I was broaching a touchy area but wanted to know how he felt before we left. I knew he was concerned about Ray and the extra burden on me. He also didn't want unpleasantness in the children's presence. I worried how he, Mom, and Father would fare after we left.

"He hasn't changed." Dad mused with a little smile. "He tries too hard and doesn't listen when you say no. But, he's a good man and always means well. He's been good for the family. Anyway, there's no sense trying any more. He'll outlive me. Damnedest thing how something simple can so quickly get out of hand for him."

"Mostly with you, it seems. I think he's happy to be with you and so willing to help, he pushes too much," I agreed, "and the tasks he jumps into are far from anything he's used to tackling. Maybe you might intimidate him a little."

"Ha! I haven't before", he said with a chuckle. "We're too old for that and haven't so many sharp edges. Mom and I know him as a good friend and like having him here."

Dad put out his cigarette on a stone and kept the butt in his hand to discard in the trash. He still smoked Camels in their soft pack with the so familiar camel and pyramid.

"Are you okay?" I asked.
"Yes. I'm fine." he said.

I marveled at this acceptance and lesson in tolerance! It was surprising how quickly he made peace with this mess. Father and he had years of history, and Dad's affection for him was evident. He respected the life of sacrifice and dedication to others that defined this man. I know he helped him with donations whenever Father had a cause he was grappling with.

I could leave without worry. We spent the rest of the dawn hour strolling the dock and yard silently. It was peaceful and beautiful. He said each morning at about this time a coral snake would make its way to the concrete apron of the dock to catch the first warming rays. As if on cue he pointed to the colorful viper emerging from the undergrowth as though to say good morning. We watched it a few minutes and then he led me quietly but quickly away. Mom complained that he captured any scorpion on the property and escorted it across the highway to the wooded area there. He was enjoying the gifts of this place after so many years of overwork and worry. He had time to notice and appreciate the little things that belonged there as much as he. I understood how much he valued the peace this paradise provided and why he wouldn't let anything even devastation to his home upend him. He showed his vulnerability with issues concerning Mom and his children and grandchildren only.

I raised his hand and pressed it to my face. He has given us so much.

After Mass, I spent a few moments with Father. He thanked me again for the wonderful fishing trip which he said had been a lifelong dream and regretted deeply Ray's injury. He worried about my doing all the driving back to Rhode Island trailing the boat and offered to try to arrange joining us to help. He was also ashamed of how the house problem had developed and welled up when he said how he hopes Dad would be able to get it all sorted out easily. I reassured him that Dad was okay and already busily arranging repairs. I told him Dad and Mom held him in a special place in their hearts and valued him as a dear friend and confidante. This friendship of so many years was special for them.

Mom and I had breakfast outside together, and she sent gifts and messages home to all my sibs and had some usual counsel for me about my family. Always her advice was to stay true to my faith and cultivate a good neighbor to call on in need. She wasn't concerned about the house situation either.

"Your Dad needs projects. Can't sit still, and the bigger the project, the more he likes it", she said. "And, I think he gets lonely for male company at times. This will have the place crawling with that company for weeks. I'll hear him laugh with them often, I'm sure."

Chapter 22

By noon we had finished packing. Next came that part of any dhow excursion that I had been dreading. Even on a newly installed public boat ramp at high tide, loading the boat on the trailer was a tense, iffy maneuver. Ray was dressed and outside. We tried to plan how this could be done without his help. Usually I would back the car and trailer down the ramp into the water, and he would guide the boat and winch and clamp it securely on the cradle. He could neither drive, guide, nor winch. Dad's steep concrete ramp ran just a couple of feet to the edge of the sandy beach. The tide was high but left most of the sand to be dealt with. The car's rear wheels could only go as far as the end of the grass and the few feet of concrete apron that kept the car's hitch quite high. Also, the boat could not approach the ramp directly as the water was too shallow there. We would have to detach and wheel the trailer down the beach at a right angle to the ramp and load the boat there. Then we would drag the boat on the trailer in the sand to the bottom of the ramp. Dad and Father were to pull the trailer, and John and Rachel were to push. Against everyone's strong objections, Ray would try to help push. I would drive.

Everyone had their instructions. I backed the car down the ramp and held it there. I was to gun the engine on Ray's signal that they had reached the hitch and snapped the trailer to it. Wheeling the empty trailer to the boat went smoothly as did loading the boat and securing it in place. Pulling it all to the car without Ray, however, was nearly impossible in that sand. I shut the engine off, and Mom and I went to help pull and push. We managed to get it to the bottom of the ramp, but still at an angle to the car. I started the car again and prepared to take off as soon as signaled. After several unsuccessful tries, it was determined that the car hitch was angled too high to make a clean, easy connection with the trailer coupling.

A strategy was devised by Dad and Ray that involved my moving the car back until the hitch was no longer at a severe slant but that gave me no room for slippage. I must hold the tires steady and gun it as I had done when learning to drive a standard transmission with a red light at the top of the hill—one foot on the clutch and one on the gas trying to hold the car in place. That had been many years ago. Automatic transmissions had spoiled my technique.

Dad stationed John and Rachel in the back pushing again, and he and Father were to take the trailer on each side of the beam that had the coupling device. On his cue they were to run up the small ramp. Because of the angle of the boat to the car, they needed to turn the trailer to the left at the same time. Dad repeated Father's role to "run to the left." The first attempt was a failure. They hadn't gotten the boat up far enough. On the second attempt something went awfully wrong. Someone who should have gone left went right, and Father and Dad butted heads so hard that Dad was knocked several feet throwing him on his back into the brackish water area at the edge of the beach. He got up looking like a sea monster ready to destroy mankind. He had vines in his hair and was soaked. He came at Father with his fists clenched and fire in his eyes. I could barely make out his words, but they were vehement. I jumped out of the car and went to help him.

"I'll kill him. So help me, I should have shot him years ago. Son of a bitch! Get out of my way." He sputtered.

He had a big red spot on his forehead. His shoes squished as he moved. This was it. He finally blew. God help Father. Thank God there was no gun handy. Mom and Ray were holding Father back from going to Dad's aid. Dad stopped and straightened up. He looked at all of us in turn shaking his head. Then he mumbled a little tightly clenched teeth laugh. We were astonished but not comfortable enough to join him. He wouldn't let me tidy him but walked over to the trailer and stood at his assigned side but didn't look at Father who walked over and picked up his side. This time with a groan of pain Ray helped lift and pull, John and Rachel pushed, and I gunned the engine at the right time to complete the maneuver. Nothing was said afterward. Dad disappeared into the house.

We loaded the luggage into the boat, added items Mom wanted taken to Rhode Island, filled the rest of the boat with coconuts and securely tied the boat cover in place. Dad had changed his clothes and composed himself. The lump on his forehead was noticeable.

Mom had helped organize the sandwiches and other provisions for the long ride home. We gathered on the front drive for a final photo and tearful hugs. This trip had been an adventure from beginning to end.

We were ready to go home. However, the drive loomed full of possibilities for yet more excitement and adventure. Ray insisted that we not cancel our Disney World plans and winced and grimaced bravely through the children's enjoyable visit there.　Leaving these three special people standing shoulder to shoulder on the driveway that day had been very hard.

They looked so much older and more vulnerable against the mounds of dirt as a backdrop. Father would stay on for a few more days. I missed and worried about each of them.

Chapter 23

We didn't make it back down to the Keys again. Dad and Mom both had health issues and decided that it was time to move back to Rhode Island.

Watching Daddy try to adjust was difficult. Often we would find him sitting in a darkened living room smoking a cigarette alone and quiet. It was determined that he required coronary artery bi-pass surgery. He did not want the surgery or to put himself in the hands of others. He didn't like that kind of attention or tampering with nature. His surgery was delayed while drug therapy was tried.

Concurrently Ray had a massive heart attack in 1979 and was given no chance of survival. He was kept alive on machines and could not be weaned off them. However, a vascular surgeon in Boston had an experimental device which he had been waiting for the right patient to try. He gave Ray no chance without it and three percent with the surgery and device. Ray agreed and four months later left Mass. Gen. Hosp. a very weak but alive man.

Dad visited him in the Surgical Intensive Care unit and was horrified. He told me to stop playing God and to let Ray die. He considered these efforts barbaric. Sadly, I think this may have had an influence on Dad's attitude toward his own upcoming surgery. However, he entered Rhode Island Hospital and submitted to the ordeal. He died on the table when he suffered an infarction under the eyes of the surgeon. Nothing could be done to save him. He was 76 years old.

Ray followed him a year later after slipping into a coma. The device had been compromised during one of his hospital stays and could not be repaired. He hoped for a transplant all along but was not a candidate after the incident. He never thought he would die. He was 50 years old.

To say these were tragic losses for all of us is insufficient. These two men were so dearly loved and needed. However, there was life to manage and children to parent. There was some comfort in our numbers and plenty of support. Mom struggled with loneliness but had our constant attention.

Father wrote lovingly to us and was obviously shaken. His faith that Dad and Ray were being rewarded for their good lives softened his loss. He did come back to visit shortly after. I was not there when he saw Mom but heard it was an emotional reunion.

He came to Narragansett to see me and the children. He looked very old and worn. His hug was as tight as ever and his eyes as bright and teary. We cried together. I cut his hair, and he looked around my old Victorian for things he might do to help. I appreciated his wanting to help very much. When we bought the house it came with a very large bag of keys, old keys of every sort. There were doors which could not be closed or locked or unlocked. He agreed to look the situation over, and we went through the house and tried the keys. He managed to match up and fix many of them. We spent a lovely afternoon together in quiet talk. He was obviously still very shaken about Dad's death but accepting. After dinner he tried to give me $20 and said he would try to send more. We played hide/find the money game which got us both laughing. I knew I would lose even after lying to him that I had no need for any more money. I promised to have a Mass offered for Dad and Ray.

We continued our correspondence and occasionally he would include some money. I knew he was juggling his limited resources and the many people he wanted to help who needed it more than I. On his gift days, I would send him a check for specific intentions on my behalf. I think he complied. His unselfishness, unconditional love, and dedication to help anywhere he could was a force to witness. His work with the poor of Detroit was taking a toll on him. He had no car and would walk or bus to those in need through winter cold and summer heat in his worn black suit and shoes and Roman collar. Like Dad he never was interested in clothes, and his suit was shiny from age and pressing.

Father helps untangle the key problem.

Chapter 24

The investment management company that Ray and I began before his death took a great deal of time and effort to close. Without his Securities and Exchange Commission registration, it was necessary for me to divest the company of all clients and responsibility for their funds. We had also begun a venture capital arm of the company, and this is where I concentrated my efforts with that of two new partners. One project required massive machinery for handling and moving materials through the manufacturing process. The largest company for this type of machinery is the Jervis B. Webb Corp. located in Detroit. Their interest in the project resulted in an invitation to visit the Detroit facility and discuss their possible involvement. They sent the company jet to North Central Airport for us. It was to be a one-night visit which didn't allow much time to see Father. However, we arranged that he would come to my hotel which he said was nearby and have coffee at 7 on the morning after my arrival.

I dressed for the day of business meetings in a black conservative outfit and waited in the lobby before 7. This hotel was new and obviously catered to short term stays by business travelers. Floor to ceiling unadorned windows filled three sides of the large two-story lobby. Elevators and the reception desk filled the fourth. The floor was shiny black marble with chrome and black leather sofas, chairs, and coffee tables on colorful round carpets scattered about to create comfortable and relatively private spaces.

Through the lobby's large windows and the dreary daylight, I saw his black hat and topcoat approaching about a block away where he had gotten off a local bus. The cold wind whipped at his hat and top coat. There were no other buildings nearby. The hotel was obviously the first to be build in a new plan for the district. The whole area had been razed, and chain link fences enclosed the vacant lots. It was a raw and dark morning. He moved swiftly with head and shoulders thrust forward and a determined stride. He looked on a mission.

When he entered the lobby, he straightened up and beamed a beautiful smile and chuckled his gravely greeting. He hugged me tightly and cried. He mumbled something about missing Dad and asked how Mom and I were managing.

We sat in chairs arranged around a coffee table in one of the areas located almost in the center of this very modern glass lobby, but it wasn't very private. Business men arrived or were checking out at the busy reception desk nearby.

I filled him in on Mom and everyone and asked him not to worry about me. Rachel and John were doing well in school, and I would be able to look for a new job soon, I hoped.

We had coffee and a warm exchange when all too soon, it was time for him to go. It was Daddy he wanted to talk about. He reminisced about things they had shared and marveled at his strong and good character and how hard and stoically he had worked. I told him of how angry Dad was with me when he visited Ray in the hospital and his words about playing God and about removing the life support machines to let him die. Father understood.

I told him of Dad's request for privacy in a letter to us that we "…make sure that there will be no more publicity, picture…than there was when Homer, our dog, passed away." He went on to say that he expected this request to be followed or "I'll get permission to come back and raise holy hell with the Journal-Bulletin and anyone else who does not comply." Father thought that very much

Dad's way. However, the Journal did honor him with a notice and data from their files.

Since then the Journal has had difficult times and been sold. There are obvious reasons for this, of course, but it amuses me to think Dad may have had some part in it.

Father tsk-tsk'ed fondly and shook his head when he said how much he missed him. He said he had enormous respect for how Dad and Mom had lived their lives. He understood when I told him that Mom had begun to keen at Dad's wake and to rock in her seat. He said he had seen this depth of sorrow many times. It was our first, but we understood immediately that it emanated from some primitive level. Father said how appreciative he was and how much our family had meant to him for all those years. He hugged me again. Then to my embarrassment, he tried to put money in my hand or pocket or anywhere he could as I resisted.

He said, "Please let me help you."

It must have been a strange sight to our interested audience. Again I knew I would lose. He squeezed my hands tightly and turned to walk away. He had his ministry to attend to this day of providing any temporal aid he was capable of with his gentle, devout spiritual assistance lovingly administered on the side. I followed a short distance knowing it was the last time I would see him. But by the way he lowered his head into the wind and moved quickly down the street, he showed clearly that he had important things he had to do that day which would keep him here in Detroit for many years to come.

Like Dad and Mom he guided his life to the end as might be done with a perfectly executed deep space launch that sails unerringly through time to that which awaits us all.

Epilogue

Father was born in Ohio on Nov. 1, 1900, to Joseph and Ada May Sherer. She was an artist and sent a large oil painting of peonies in a vase to Mom in appreciation of our friendship and love for her son. Mom gave it place of pride in her home over the mantle.

After prep school, Father entered the novitiate of St. Joseph's Province and Priory in Ohio, and was ordained in Washington, DC, in 1930. He received a Master of Science Degree in 1933. He was assigned to Providence College that year and then to a stint in Washington, D.C., until 1941. At this time he returned to Providence College and taught chemistry and physics until 1950.

After an assignment for 15 years in Columbus, Ohio, he spent the next 28 years of his priesthood at St. Dominic's Parish in Detroit, Michigan. His failing health brought him in 1993 to the Province's Center for Assisted Living in Washington and later to an infirmary in New Jersey.

His relatives requested that he spend the last year of his life in Fresno, California, where he died in 1996 at age 95. He was eulogized by the Provincial of his order and is buried in Benicia, California, in the order's Dominican Cemetery.

In his last will to the friars of his order St. Dominic said, "Behold, my children, the heritage I leave you: have charity, guard humility, and make your treasure out of voluntary poverty." That legacy was Father's life. He will be remembered for his zeal in helping the poor and destitute and by the title bestowed on him by the people of Detroit of "Apostle of the Poor".

In his last letter to me dated June 6, 1995, Father describes how his physical condition requires his going to a facility which is better equipped to provide his needs. It is telling that he describes his condition as the physical. His mind and soul were as vibrant and dedicated as ever.

He says, "About six months ago they took my highball away and I lost my appetite. Not eating I lost my strength." He speaks of his new location as, "I can make new friends and I hope do some good there before my departure. I will always be delighted to hear from you, or better to see your smiling face. I love you and beg our Dear Lord to love and bless you."

Many of the moments recounted here have a humorous element. They are but a few among the countless peaceful and happy times spent with these three wonderful people.

To live a rewarding and valuable experience before our time comes, we may simply follow in their footsteps. The moral code and value system that they not only lived but espoused is invaluable in these troubled times. Dad's single word judgment, "Nonsense", is still powerful and valuable. The least that is asked of us is that we share with our children what has been given to us. As Father said, selfishness is corrupting and unworthy. He relentlessly tried to teach us a way of life worthy of a saintly reward, and Dad and Mom provided an example for us to witness. I thank them and God for their love and guidance.

The Rev. Joseph M. Sherer was a livelong figure of friendship, comfort, and guidance in our lives. This loving biography of him covers only those days in his dynamic career during which he was available to us and does not represent the totality of his years and priesthood. This memoir is inspired by the relevance and persistence of recollections of the past and affectionate respect for him.

For the Love of Pete and Fr. Schnapps

Rareripes Group
P. O. Box 8787
Cranston, Rhode Island 02920

ISBN-13: 978-0692795798
ISBN-10: 0692795790
Library of Congress Catalog Number: 2016917452

Manufactured in the United States
Digital format by Ivy Road Design